child LABOR

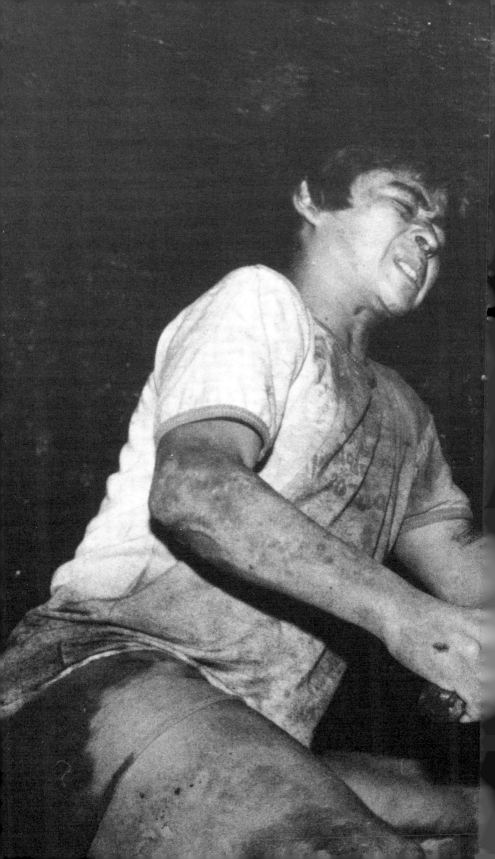

child
LABOR

A GLOBAL CRISIS
KATHLYN GAY

The Millbrook Press
Brookfield, Connecticut

Photographs courtesy of Impact Visuals: pp. 2-3
(© 1995 Meredith Davenport), 37 (© Johan Berglund), 51
(© Meredith Davenport), 81 (© Rommel Pecson); AP/Wide
World Photos: pp. 15, 34, 61, 69, 96; Gamma Liaison: pp. 24
(© Robert Nickelsberg), 41 (© Andres Hernandez)

Published by The Millbrook Press, Inc.
2 Old New Milford Road
Brookfield, Connecticut 06804

Copyright © 1998 by Kathlyn Gay
All rights reserved
Printed in the United States of America
5 4 3 2 1

Library of Congress Cataloging-in-Publication Data
Gay, Kathlyn
Child labor: a global crisis/Kathlyn Gay.
p. cm.
Includes bibliographical references and index.
Summary: Examines child-labor practices throughout the world within a
  historical context and discusses ways of dealing with the problem.
ISBN 0-7613-0368-5 (lib. bdg.)
1. Children—Employment—History—Juvenile literature.
2. Children—Employment—Law and legislation. 3. Child welfare.
[1. Children—Employment. 2. Child welfare. 3. Child abuse.]
I. Title.
HD6231.G39 1998   98—17670   CIP   AC
331.3'4'09—dc21

CONTENTS

child LABOR

CHAPTER 1

WHAT IS
child LABOR?

When she was eleven years old, Nazma Akhter began work in Bangladesh's garment industry as a helper for sewing-machine operators. Eventually she became an operator herself and earned an equivalent of $15 per month. "I was working in the factory from 8 A.M. to midnight seven days a week," she said.[1]

Today Akhter is on the staff of a garment workers' union, urging better conditions and pay for workers. She explained that when she was a seamstress in the factory, most of the employees were young women and girls. She estimates "at least 30 percent of the workers were under the age of fourteen." Children were able to work in the factories because they "were considered desirable employees . . . they followed orders, were too timid to complain, were unlikely to assert their rights. . . . Children could also be easily intimidated with physical punishment for making mistakes. I was personally beaten when I made mistakes or when I was late for work."[2]

The young workers in the Bangladesh garment industry represent just one type of child labor—that which occurs in "sweatshops." The term sweatshop stems from the poorly ventilated, unsanitary, and hazardous factories that were common in the United States during the late 1800s and early 1900s. Sweatshops still exist in the United States and are commonplace in many other countries, particularly in so-called developing nations. In some sweatshops, workers are captive children.

In India, for example, eight-year-old Laxmi Sada was kidnapped and taken to a carpet factory to work. Laxmi told a *Boston Globe* reporter: "Me and three more boys were playing outside the village, and some people came and gave us something to eat and said they had even better things to eat. They took us in a bus. I didn't even know what a carpet factory was. I started crying. Many times I was beaten. It was the master who first hit me with the *punja* (a comblike tool), and the blood came down . . . then they would put matchstick powder on the wound and light it to stop the bleeding. I never saw the sun rise."[3]

Like thousands of others working under such cruel conditions, Laxmi could not even get up to go to the bathroom. "If you got up, you'd get beaten," he said. Laxmi's father tried to rescue him, but he was attacked by factory thugs. "I saw my father being beaten," Laxmi told the reporter. "He could not recover. My father wanted to take me and put me on his lap."[4]

Factories make up only a small percentage of the places where child workers toil and sweat, suffer brutal treatment, or face health and safety hazards. Most of the world's working kids are not in the formal sector—established businesses and industries. Rather they work in the informal sector in private homes, in agricultural fields, or on the street.

Consider Celine (not her real name), who was only ten years old when her family in Haiti sent her from their rural home to the city of Port-au-Prince. A businessman had made the arrangements, promising Celine's parents that their daughter would be able to go to school and have a chance for a life beyond that of the utter poverty that most of the peasants in Haiti endure. But as has been the case for tens of thousands of other young Haitian *restaviks* (a word from the French meaning "to stay with"), Celine's employers had no intention of sending her to school—until a Catholic priest in Port-au-Prince persuaded them to do otherwise.

Even though Celine, now a teenager, has been able to attend school, she also has had to spend long hours at domestic work. As she told a reporter: "The sun is not up when I get up. I wash the dishes. I iron. I cook. I clean the plates people have eaten off. I fill buckets with water. I work for a household of five, including me. The parents of the family work as a mechanic and as a seamstress." She also revealed that the mother of the family she works for frequently beats her, a common practice among such employers.[5]

At the age of eleven, Elionardo began work in Brazil's sugarcane fields. Sugar and other products refined from sugarcane are a major export and provide high profits for growers and a multibillion-dollar U.S. corporation, Archer-Daniels Midland, which produces corn sweeteners, biochemicals, and ethanol—a corn-based alcohol used for fuel. But workers in the fields earn very little.

"It is a bad job. You leave very early in the morning and come back home at 5 P.M. There is a risk of getting your leg cut, getting hurt. You get all dirty, you starve, and you get home very late," Elionardo explained.[6] Elionardo was able to leave the sugarcane fields by becoming part of a United Nations Children's Fund (UNICEF) program that provides an allowance for child laborers to go to school and to "eat dinner," as he put it.

Stories like those of Nazma, Laxmi, Celine, and Elionardo could be repeated millions of times over. Worldwide an estimated 250 million children between the ages of five and fourteen are working in developing countries. Many of these children are enslaved or bonded laborers— turned over to employers to work and pay off debts owed by family members, according to a 1996 survey by the International Labor Organization (ILO). The ILO says its count of child laborers is undoubtedly low, since there is no precise system for gathering statistics on a global scale. In most countries surveys of the labor force rarely include illegal, concealed, or home-based work.[7]

CHILD WORK VS. CHILD LABOR

For centuries, everywhere in the world, children in poor families have worked to help keep themselves and their family members alive. Even when survival is not at stake, children in middle-class and affluent families may be encouraged to get jobs because employment during childhood can bring economic, social, and personal benefits. Kids work in order to learn skills, to develop discipline and self-esteem, and to understand the value of money.

It is also a tradition in many families for children to work in family enterprises, such as on a farm or in a business. Marcy Abramson Shoemaker of Philadelphia is an example. When she was an adolescent she worked in her father's packaged-gift business. She explained: "I took an apple, put tissue paper around it and put the boxes together, and put the apples in the boxes . . . and I did that eight to ten hours a day."[8] Shoemaker's early experiences helped her develop discipline and work skills that later enabled her to become a successful entrepreneur and launch her own business in the Philadelphia area.

Another common work practice is for young people to get jobs because they want to have their own spending money or they hope to save for college or for a special purchase, such as a bicycle, roller blades, or perhaps a car. To that end, countless adolescents and teenagers have found paid work delivering newspapers, mowing lawns, shoveling snow, baby-sitting, shopping, and doing similar tasks. This work usually is not destructive and does not prevent a child from going to school or getting needed rest.

Obviously, the option to work at such jobs is quite different from having no choice at all in such matters. Because of extreme poverty in developing nations, parents frequently force their children into jobs that threaten their physical development, their long-term health, and even their lives. Many children worldwide labor seven days a week at jobs that cripple them, stunt their growth, or damage them emotionally.

Since about 1990, numerous individuals and international groups have drawn attention to the types of child labor that exploit children. To exploit, in simple terms, means to use a person for selfish reasons, to take advantage of someone for profit. Because children in most poor countries have little if any power, employers can control them through abuse (beatings and torture) and force them to work under abominable conditions. Exploitation also occurs when children at a very young age are prevented from going to school and compelled to work long hours for pay that is far less than adults earn for the same work. "The younger the child, the lower the wage," ILO reports.[9]

In defining exploitative child labor, UNICEF declares that it involves:

- full-time work at too early an age
- too many hours spent working
- work that exerts undue physical, social, or psychological stress
- work and life on the streets in bad conditions
- inadequate pay
- too much responsibility
- work that hampers access to education
- work that undermines children's dignity and self-esteem, such as slavery or bonded labor and sexual exploitation
- work that is detrimental to social and psychological development[10]

Exploitative child labor, then, is the issue at hand. But it is a complex issue, especially when some exploited children themselves insist that they must work to survive. The issue is complicated further because in numerous countries rich and poor alike consider child labor to be acceptable, a "natural condition" that is the result of poverty.

Rajesh Sahani, age fourteen, falls asleep standing up after twelve hours of road building in Pokhara, India. Rajesh has never been to school. Hard labor is his past, his present, and his future.

WORLDWIDE SCOPE OF CHILD LABOR

People in industrialized nations tend to believe that children are exploited only in poor countries, but hazardous and destructive forms of child labor can be found in every nation, including the United States. Each year, the U.S. Department of Labor (DOL) cites numerous cases of minors working illegally in dangerous occupations.[11] However, most of the world's exploited children live in Asia, Africa, and Latin America, according to UNICEF's 1997 *State of the World's Children*, an annual report. While half of those children are in Asia, one child out of every three is at work in Africa, and one child in five works in Latin America. In both Africa and Latin America, only a very small percentage of child workers are employed in established businesses and industries. The vast majority work for their families, in homes as servants, in the fields, or they sell or beg in the streets, the report states.[12]

The largest number of urban and rural child workers in the world are in India, according to the DOL. While the Indian government "acknowledges at least 17.5 million working children," other estimates by nongovernmental groups and some international organizations "range from 44 million to over 100 million child workers," the DOL states. "Major export industries which utilize child labor include hand-knotted carpets, gemstone polishing, brass and base metal articles, glass and glassware, footwear, textiles and silk, and fireworks." Other industries in India that allegedly use child labor include slate mining and quarrying, furniture making, and food processing, reports the DOL.[13]

Child laborers are also used in the export industries of many other countries. One example is Colombia, where children work in flower fields. Carnations, roses, lilies, and other flowers are grown for export primarily to the United States and European countries. One young worker said that growers "like to employ children because we have small hands and can work fast."[14] The *World Press Review* reported that in Bogotá young children are picked up every morning and taken by bus to the farms. A doctor working with a social-welfare group in Bogotá said that children eight or nine years old mix pesticides "without gloves, masks, or any protection. We may not see the effects until five to twenty years later when they can no longer move their hands. Many farms use very dangerous organochlorides," toxins that are banned in many countries because they cause "disruption of the central nervous system leading to paralysis or epilepsy" and other diseases such as cancer.[15]

Tanya began work in the flower fields at the age of thirteen, and at fifteen she reported: "I get dizzy and faint. My stomach hurts. Sometimes I feel as if I'm drunk. My vision goes and I can't stand up."[16]

Young agricultural workers in Mexico face similar hazards as they toil in crews with their parents, harvesting tomatoes, onions, and other field crops. In many other Mexican industries, children "can be found gluing shoes in workshops . . . stacking bricks . . . lifting two or three times their body weight in produce," and cleaning up toxic oil wastes, according to *U.S. News & World Report*. "The work performed by many kids leaves them scarred, injured, or disabled."[17]

UNICEF cites similar hazardous work conditions around the world. For example, "In Malaysia, children may work up to seventeen-hour days on rubber plantations, exposed to insect and snake bites. In the United Republic of Tanzania, they pick coffee, inhaling pesticides. In Portugal, children as young as twelve are subject to the heavy labor and myriad dangers of the construction industry. In Morocco, they hunch at looms for long hours and little pay, knotting the strands of luxury carpets for export."[18]

Wherever children are exploited, they work because they or their families need the money. But poverty is not the only reason they are deprived of an education and forced to labor. Child-labor practices in many countries are rooted in traditions that are centuries old.

CHAPTER 2

WHY
child LABOR?

Although poor families in many parts of the world depend on the small income a child laborer may contribute, that income does little or nothing to help a family escape dire poverty. Instead, the earnings frequently mean the difference between starvation and bare subsistence, since parents of most child laborers are unemployed or are employed only part-time or occasionally. Obviously, adults in developing countries desperately need work. However, the jobs are offered to children, because child laborers can be paid less than adults. Employers thus exploit children as a means of increasing their profits.

When adults cannot get jobs at wages that help them sustain their families, the cycle of poverty goes on. Children who work instead of going to school have little chance to find jobs that will help increase their income. If children are forced to work in conditions that damage them physically and emotionally, their prospects are even worse for a better life. The UNICEF report *State of the World's Children* put it this way: "Poverty begets child labor begets lack of education begets poverty."[1]

THE REAL FACE
OF POVERTY

Yet it is no easy matter for millions of child laborers to get an education and to break the poverty cycle, as a group of reporters for Children's Express (CE) learned in 1996 when they traveled to Bangladesh. CE is a nonprofit children's news service organized to train children and teenagers nationwide to be reporters and editors. The purpose of CE's trip, which was sponsored by the United Nations, was to learn firsthand about child labor. Thirteen-year-old Josh Kretman of Washington, D.C., was with the team and reported:

> *We interviewed one girl who earned the equivalent of 25 cents for a 12-hour day, breaking batteries. She worked among carbon and battery acid every day. Kids as young as five worked with her. She said that if she could change her life in any way, she would want to work in a garment factory. Hearing a girl of about eleven years old say that she wanted to work in a factory really put things into perspective for me.*
>
> *I always thought that working in a factory at such an early age would be one of the worst things imaginable. Before researching child-labor issues with my reporting team, I thought that, of course, every child should be taken out*

of factories and put in school. After traveling half way around the world and seeing unbelievable poverty, I now know that the solution is not that simple. In some countries, such as Bangladesh, if poor kids are not working in factories, they are likely to be put out in the streets, either begging or working in more physically dangerous jobs. For these children, it is not a matter of working to live well and eat three meals a day in a nice home. The children must make a choice of either working, starving or perhaps even dying.[2]

Through interpreters the CE team talked to other young people in Bangladesh and posted their stories on the internet, helping to draw attention to the poverty that is one cause of child labor in that and other countries. Jalil, about eleven, said that he "used to work in a garment factory. My parents sent me there. I've got a blind father who begs. My mother accompanies him. I've got two brothers and one sister. My sister is married. She is about twenty to twenty-two years old. She's got a son. My house is a big room that is shared by about twenty to twenty-four people."[3]

The effects of poverty were also described by ten former child laborers who took part in a fall 1997 conference called the Children's Forum in Bangkok, Thailand. For two days prior to the main conference, young people held a workshop to prepare statements on child labor and explain how poverty forced them to work at an early age. They came from Cambodia, Indonesia, Mongolia, the Philippines, and Thailand.

Among the participants was seventeen-year-old Taliinsar Dorjiin of Mongolia, who said: "My family was very poor and sometimes we would not find anything to eat. My father's salary was very low and we could not supply oneself in ordinary conditions. So I came to the street and tried to make my own life." Out on the street Taliinsar could not find a job and with friends turned to picking pockets to get money. Sometimes they gathered "foods from the garbage in case we could not find any money." However, with the help of a policeman, Taliinsar was able to join a program designed to aid street kids and save them from "child labor in the streets" and a life of crime.[4]

A young girl in the Philippines declared that she has not enjoyed her childhood "because at the age of thirteen I left my home and started working as a domestic helper . . . . My employer is a relative. I start working at 6 o'clock in the morning, do all housework: cleaning, washing, baby-sitting. I work until 10 in the evening. My employer don't give me salary and clothes. Because my employer's house is very big, I have a lot of work to do. The glass-windows of house are large and high. So it is difficult for me to clean. I am still going to school on Sundays, run by a church for poor children. I want employer to pay salary to me so that I have money to learn more."[5]

DIVERSE ATTITUDES ABOUT CHILD LABOR

Cultural influences play a major role in attitudes about child labor. In some countries, ideas about the kinds of activities that are appropriate for children (as well as adults) are based on the caste system. This system categorizes people from birth into economic groups ranging from a ruling upper class to a low class almost as powerless as slaves. In Pakistan, for example, the children of the lowest castes "become laborers almost as soon as they can walk," according to a report in *Atlantic Monthly*. "Much of the nation's farmland is worked by toddlers, yoke teams of three-, four-, and five-year olds who plough, seed, and glean fields from dawn to dusk. On any given morning the canal banks and irrigation ditches in rural villages are lined with urchins who stand no taller than the piles of laundry they wash for their wealthier neighbors."[6]

The caste system is well established in India, leading to a high rate of child exploitation. According to a UNICEF report, some owners of bonded laborers believe that low-caste children should work rather than go to school. "Once they are allowed to come up to an equal level, nobody will go to the fields. Fields will be left uncultivated everywhere. We have to keep them under our strong thumb in order to get work done," one owner said.[7]

Another practice that exploits poor and low-caste Indian children is using them in the alms business—as beggars. Parents of young children, many of them deformed (in some cases deliberately crippled), send their young sons or daughters with relatives or other agents to rich countries like Saudi Arabia. There "rich people donate generously to the poor," as one mother explained. Parents are promised the equivalent of about $500 from the alms business, but they usually get only part of the money. The agents get the major portion.[8]

A worker at a brick factory in Pakistan. Children are involved in every phase of production at this factory. The only adults are supervisors who are not there to ensure the children's safety but rather to make sure that the quotas are met each day.

In many countries around the world, children born into a poor family may be considered fit only for full-time work. Some families may even have children in order to increase the number of workers and their family income. Such children frequently work with their families on farms where vegetables and fruits are grown, usually for export and domestic markets. Or they work on plantations with their families. Most of these plantations are located in tropical or subtropical regions, and hired workers cultivate and produce marketable crops such as bananas, coconuts, coffee, cotton, tobacco, tea, palm oil, pineapples, and rice. The ILO reports that about 20 million people work on plantations in various countries and "hundreds of thousands of children" are part of that workforce. In fact, more children worldwide are employed in agriculture than in any other industry.[9]

Children are recruited for farm or plantation work to perform tasks their parents prefer not to do, or they care for younger brothers and sisters while their parents work. In some cases mothers take their children to work with them in the fields because there is no available or safe child care. Some children work in agriculture to earn their own income.[10]

Lack of understanding about the importance of education is another factor that propels young people into the labor force. Poor parents may believe that children are better off at home learning a skill that will help improve the family income. Even when families want their children to be educated, schools may be nonexistent or too far away or too expensive for children to attend. In addition, schools in many areas of poor countries (and

also in impoverished areas of wealthy nations) are over-crowded and frequently hazardous to health and safety. Teachers are not well trained and are indifferent or abusive; their attitudes may reflect their cultural prejudices against youngsters who are from low-class or poor families. All of these factors cause children to drop out of school and go to work.

GENDER DISCRIMINATION

Gender is a major consideration in whether a child is forced to work. While boys are more visible in workforces around the world, girls in developing countries may be trained to do unpaid household chores and care for younger children so that others in their families can get paid jobs. Worldwide "more girls than boys are denied their fundamental right to primary schooling," UNICEF reports. In Nepal, for example, the overwhelming majority of girls either have never gone to school or have dropped out to work. "Discrimination soon becomes exploitation. Lack of education, early arranged marriages, stark poverty, and lack of power make girls enormously vulnerable. Long before they are physically prepared for it, many are forced to work, most of them ending up, if not in domestic service then in the carpet industry, on tea estates, or in brickmaking."[11]

All over the developing world, gender discrimination creates a demeaning cycle for girls. Girls who cannot attend school because they come from a low-status social group or because they are forced to work at home "are denied the extra power and wider horizons that education would bring. If they seek work outside the home, their opportunities are limited to the most menial tasks. Their low status is reinforced and passed on to the next generation," UNICEF states.[12]

In some countries girls have so little value that parents sell them off for prostitution, or girls are routinely kidnapped (with little chance of escape or police protection) for use in the sex industry.

LAX CHILD-LABOR LAWS

Virtually every country in the world has national laws that limit the extent to which children may be employed and set requirements for attending school. Most nations also bar children from hazardous work, or work that interferes with their education, damages their health, or harms their physical, mental, spiritual, or moral development. Nevertheless, such laws are seldom enforced, according to reports by the Bureau of International Labor Affairs (ILAB) of the U.S. Department of Labor.

In 1993 the U.S. Congress mandated that the ILAB conduct a study to identify foreign industries that use child labor in the manufacture or mining of products that are exported to the United States. A second study authorized the following year deals with the use of child labor in agricultural imports and forced and bonded child labor. Findings from these studies were published in two reports titled *By the Sweat and Toil of Children* (Volumes I and II). A third study in 1996 focused on the apparel industry and international child-labor problems.

The Bureau of International Labor Affairs found that "governments, especially in the developing world, lack an adequate system for obtaining accurate data on child labor. Moreover, they are reluctant to document activities which are often illegal under their domestic laws, violate international labor standards, and are perceived by many as a serious failure in their public policy."[13]

Dozens of International Labor Organization Conventions (agreements) and other international treaties pertain to child labor and set guidelines for national laws and policies to eliminate the exploitation of children. The 1989 United Nations Convention on the Rights of the Child (CRC) is one such international agreement that includes broad measures to protect children's rights. As the preamble to the convention points out, "children, because of their vulnerability, need special care and protection." It emphasizes the responsibility of the family for primary care and protection, and also "the need for legal and other protection of the child before and after birth, the importance of respect for the cultural values of the child's community, and the vital role of international cooperation in securing children's rights."[14]

Part I of the convention spells out the major provisions for ensuring children's rights. Signatory nations agree, for example, that "the child has a right to education and the State's [nation's] duty is to ensure that primary education is free and compulsory." Participants to the international agreement also "recognize the right of the child to be protected from economic exploitation and from performing any work that is likely to be hazardous or to interfere with the child's education, or to be harmful to the child's health or physical, mental, spiritual, moral, or social development."[15]

By the end of 1997, all except two members of the United Nations—the United States and Somalia—had signed the agreement. Numerous U.S. organizations support the convention, and in November 1997, U.S. Representative Bernie Sanders of Vermont introduced a bill (Rights of the Child Act of 1997) calling for ratification of the CRC. But there has been a great deal of opposition from individuals and groups who believe that the CRC takes away from national and state sovereignty and undermines parental authority.

Since 1919 the ILO has adopted twelve international agreements on child labor. One is the Minimum Age Convention of 1973, usually referred to as Convention 138. Of the 173 member countries of the ILO, only 49 have ratified or agreed to accept the convention's provisions, but more than "30 countries have started the ratification process or are considering it," according to the ILO.[16]

Each country that has ratified the convention also has attached a declaration setting a minimum age for employment or work within its territory, banning employment to anyone under that age. The minimum age specified cannot be less than that set for compulsory schooling, and, in any case, not less than fifteen years. However, a nation whose economy and educational facilities are not well developed is allowed to set the minimum age at fourteen years, and twelve years is the minimum age stipulated for "light work." The agreement also prohibits young people under the age of eighteen from work that is likely to jeopardize their health, safety, or morals, as

stated in the United Nations Convention on Children's
Rights.[17] International agreements can have considerable
impact on national legislation to protect child workers,
but child labor continues on a massive scale. Why? The
ILO explains as follows:

> *It is often condoned in silence, or justified with
> the argument that poverty makes it unavoid-
> able and that work is a useful form of prepara-
> tion for adulthood. Because it is illegal, it has
> often been declared or assumed not to exist.
> However, the wall of silence, apathy and denial
> is beginning to crumble. Within a remarkably
> short period of time, child labor has . . . become
> a high priority on the agenda of the world
> community.*[18]

EFFECTS OF
GLOBALIZATION

Since the early 1990s child labor has indeed received
global attention, primarily because of media reports
about the use of children in the production of goods
marketed by many large multinational, or global, corporations. These global companies have headquarters in
their countries of origin, but they maintain a worldwide
network of small suppliers or manufacturers, some of
which allow child labor or ignore laws against it. Thus
production costs for multinational companies can be re-
duced considerably when children do the work at lower
rates of pay than adults receive.

Around the world nations and small companies attempt to entice multinational firms to set up operations within their borders. A major lure for global firms is a low-wage workforce. When workers and organizations try to stamp out child labor or improve conditions in workplaces, a company may decide to move elsewhere. Globalization, then, has played a role in sustaining child labor. U.S.-based companies are among the global firms that have been cited for "jobbing out" the production of toys, sporting goods, rugs, clothing, footwear, and other items to overseas contractors who use child labor. Since about 1994, some investigative reports have indicated that child labor may be declining in some countries, perhaps due to widespread publicity and public pressure worldwide to eliminate the practice. On the other hand, child labor has continued unabated in some parts of the world, especially in countries where child workers are out of sight in village factories and home workplaces. The most grievous child-labor practices are those that use bonded or enslaved children to supply the global marketplace.

CHAPTER 3

BONDED AND ENSLAVED
children

Although human-rights groups, labor organizations, and many others have long called attention to the plight of bonded and enslaved child workers, a number of government studies and widespread media reports during the 1990s have focused on the inhumane conditions under which these children work. One story that has prompted student activists and others to demand an end to child labor was that of Iqbal Masih of Pakistan.

When Iqbal was four years old, his parents had to borrow the equivalent of $12 from a moneylender. To pay off their debt, Iqbal's parents turned over their son to the moneylender, who placed Iqbal in a carpet factory as a bonded laborer. Iqbal was required to work in conditions of servitude (virtual slavery) to repay his parents' debt. But like millions of other indentured, or bonded, children in Pakistan and other countries, he received little if any pay and was under complete control of a master— the manufacturer. Iqbal was chained to a carpet loom and forced to work sixteen hours a day. He and other bonded children were often starved, beaten, and tortured.

Iqbal escaped from the factory when he was ten years old and attended a meeting of the Bonded Labor Liberation Front (BLLF), where he and other escapees learned about their rights. At the gathering, Iqbal gave an impromptu speech describing the abuse he suffered. He and other child workers were often put in a punishment room if their owner disapproved of their work or if they fell asleep. Numerous times Iqbal was sent to the room, tied with a rope around his knees, and hung upside down. Other children were punished by having their fingers burned with boiling oil.

After his escape, Iqbal refused to go back to the factory. With the help of a BLLF lawyer, who cited a seldom-enforced 1992 Pakistani law prohibiting child labor, Iqbal was freed. Because of being malnourished and being immobile for hours in front of a loom, Iqbal did not develop properly and at the age of twelve was about the size of a six-year-old. But his dream was to prevent other Pakistani children from suffering the way he did.

In 1994 the International Labor Organization sponsored Iqbal's visit to an international conference in Stockholm, Sweden. Later he traveled to Boston, Massachusetts, to receive Reebok's Youth in Action award. While in Massachusetts he spoke to school groups about the horrors of forced child labor in carpet factories. He hoped to go back to his village and help build a school. But in April 1995, while riding his bike in front of his grandmother's home in Pakistan, he was shot and killed. Many speculate that the gunman was connected with the carpet manufacturers, but no one has been convicted of the murder.[1]

Class advisor Donna Willoughby shows her students an Amnesty International poster of Iqbal Masih, who was murdered after he became an activist in the fight against child labor.

Iqbal Masih's cause did not die with him, however. Students across the United States and around the world have joined in efforts to help build a school and ultimately to stop child labor, as is described in more detail in Chapter 7.

THE ASIAN CARPET INDUSTRY

Since the early 1990s activists in Western countries have been highly critical of the carpet industry in South Asia, which exports products to the United States, Canada, Japan, and European countries. Because of the negative publicity about barbaric treatment of child workers, carpet sales have dropped. Nevertheless, in countries like Pakistan and India—the nations with the largest number of child workers—the illegal practice continues, frequently ignored by authorities and the general public until recent times.

Some groups, however, have been taking action. For example, the South Asian Coalition on Child Servitude (SACCS), founded in 1980 and led by Kailash Satyarthi, has rescued more than 29,000 bonded children in India.[2] One of those liberated children was Aghan, who was taken to Satyarthi's *ashram*, or religious retreat, outside New Delhi.

Aghan had been a bonded worker for more than two years and was mutilated by his master. As a *Life* magazine reporter wrote: "[Aghan's] master branded his right cheek with a glowing iron rod, then inserted a toxin that blinded his left eye when Aghan pleaded to go home to see his mother. . . . He knows he is hard to look at and that his life, no matter how free, will never be easy." After the torture the carpet master continued to threaten Aghan, telling the boy, "If you ever remember your family again and ask to go home, I will kill you."[3]

Satyarthi, who provided information for the *Life* report, also writes articles about the abused child workers he has seen and rescued. In an essay posted on the internet, he described a rescued carpet boy, Tsleem, who was about six or seven years old and "benumbed to all human feelings. There was no trace of happiness or sorrow. But underneath his expressionless face I could feel the agony of his tender heart. I pulled him into my fold, caressed and cajoled him to break his silence and eventually he broke down. Once he got nostalgic, he wept thinking of his mother. This irritated the owner, and he hit Tsleem with a rod. With that the latter lost all human expression."[4]

BONDED CHILDREN IN OTHER INDUSTRIES

Bonded child laborers make up a significant portion of the workforce in Asian industries that produce such goods as silk thread, footwear, hand-rolled cigarettes, and jewelry. In Karnataka, center of the silk market in India, "there may be as many as 100,000 bonded children involved in every stage of silk production," according to the *Multinational Monitor*. Many begin working at the age of five producing silk thread. At the time of the *Monitor* report two boys named Ajad and Marukh were ten years old and worked as reelers. They "dip their hands into scalding water and palpate the silk cocoons, sensing

army, primarily because "they are easy to organize, and they don't ask questions. In wartime, a commander wants total submission. You get that only from a child," the *World Press Review* reported.[7]

In the Philippines, bonded children "are treated like animals. They are caged and padlocked inside jail-like structures when they are not at work. . . . They are assigned to living quarters that are congested, unventilated, filthy and smelly and that are not fit for human beings," according to a UNICEF report.[8]

Thousands of people, including many children, work in slavelike conditions in former Burma, which was taken over by the military in 1962 and renamed Myanmar. The State Law and Order Restoration Council (SLORC) of the military junta has since repressed its citizens. Human Rights Watch (HRW), a nongovernmental agency, reported in 1997 that "children are used as porters to carry supplies for the army, often resulting in exhaustion, illness and sometimes death, not only from inadequate medical care, but also from beatings."

In addition, HRW notes that in 1996 alone more than 200,000 people, many of them children and their families, have been forced to leave their homes and villages in relocation programs. In the towns and cities, children are arbitrarily arrested and detained, often without charge or trial, for as little as shouting out slogans or giving out leaflets. Throughout the country children are routinely used as unpaid laborers on government construction projects, and adoption of children is often used as a means of securing unpaid child labor in domestic service or other businesses. Many Burmese girls are trafficked into Thailand, through border checkpoints administered by the

SLORC, where they become bonded laborers often working in slavelike conditions.[9]

Children used in Burma's construction projects help build the nation's infrastructure—airports, roads, bridges, and railways. These projects are designed to develop the country's tourist trade and foster economic growth, but numerous children and adults suffer the consequences—they are worked to exhaustion or death. A British observer saw child workers who carried heavy loads of mud mixed with straw in baskets and dishes on their heads and clearly agonized under the weight.

After they poured the mixture into a vat and grinder, the sticky clay, now almost as hard as rock, was gathered by two small children, one of them small enough to fit up to his shoulders in a hole directly beneath the grinder. Horrified, I watched a load of clay, like fresh cement, tip over, almost burying him. I reached under his arms and pulled him out. The others laughed as if this was normal.[10]

HIDDEN WORKERS

While some enslaved or bonded child workers are visible to investigators, millions of children around the world work unseen in domestic service—given or sold at a very early age to another family. According to the U.S. Department of Labor, such forced child laborers "receive little or no pay and have no control over their daily lives. They are often forced to work beyond their physical capacity and under conditions that seriously threaten their health, safety and development."[11] UNICEF calls child

Girls are not exempt from hard and dangerous work. The girl on the left was not seen by a physician, nor was she given any time to recuperate from a traumatic head wound.

domestic workers "the world's most forgotten children," who "may well be the most vulnerable and exploited children of all, as well as the most difficult to protect," because they are not under public scrutiny. They often suffer severe physical and psychological damage, and because of constant intimidation may be extremely fearful, anxious, and passive, UNICEF reports.[12] Most domestics are young girls, such as Celine of Haiti described in Chapter 1. Another is seven-year-old Marie, also a Haitian *restavik*. A brief look at Marie's day is included in UNICEF's 1997 report:

She gets up at five in the morning and begins her day by fetching water from a nearby well, balancing the heavy jug on her head as she returns. She prepares breakfast and serves it to the members of the household. Then she walks the family's five-year-old son to school; later, at noon, she brings him home and helps him change clothes.

Next, she helps prepare and serve the family's lunch before returning the boy to school. In between mealtimes she must buy food in the market and run errands, tend the charcoal fire, sweep the yard, wash clothes and dishes, clean the kitchen and—at least once a day—wash her female boss's feet. She is given leftovers or cornmeal to eat, has ragged clothes and no shoes and sleeps outdoors or on the floor. She is not allowed to bathe in the water she brings to the household. She is regularly beaten with a leather strap if she is slow to respond to a request or is

*considered disrespectful. Needless to say, she is
not allowed to attend school.*[13]

A chilling story of repeated abuse of domestic worker
Dhiraj K.C.—a name given to him by his employer—
was posted on the internet by Child Workers in Nepal
(CWIN), an agency caring for abused child laborers.
Dhiraj became a live-in worker when he was seven years
old because his father was a drunkard and his mother
and one of his sisters died.

Dhiraj, who does not know his real family name, took
a younger sister to Kathmandu, where the two were employed by a man who worked for a medical company.
According to CWIN, the children were physically and
mentally abused over a period of five years. Dhiraj bore
numerous scars from being beaten with a hot iron, forced
to wear chains from his neck to his feet while he worked,
and chained naked outside all night in freezing weather.
On one occasion, the employer used a hypodermic
needle to inject an anesthetic into Dhiraj's lip, causing
numbness and preventing him from speaking. CWIN
reported that the injection was punishment for saying
angry words to the employer's son. Another time, the
employer pushed handfuls of raw chilies down Dhiraj's
throat and then forced the boy to eat boiling hot rice.

He finally escaped by crawling in chains to the streets
where he was picked up by police. Dhiraj and his sister
were eventually rescued by CWIN.[14]

Some domestic workers, especially young teenagers,
are also abused sexually. Frequently male family members believe that they are entitled to rape the girls—sexual
abuse is considered part of the servitude.

Although research on the child domestic workers is sparse, an international conference on the subject was held in Great Britain in 1996. Participants came from Bangladesh, Nepal, Indonesia, the Philippines, Kenya, Senegal, Togo, Haiti, and Guatemala. In nearly all the countries where children work as household servants, most people do not regard this practice as damaging or are unaware of the brutality that some child workers suffer. Researchers are seldom able to obtain meaningful information from child workers or their employers. Many employers refuse to allow investigators to interview their child servants on a one-to-one basis and often will not allow researchers into their homes. In short, the children are virtually invisible—out of sight and out of mind, as an old saying puts it. Thus they can be exploited for years, if not for a lifetime.

INTOLERABLE SEXUAL EXPLOITATION

One of the most brutal forms of child labor is using children in the sex industry. At least one million young girls and an uncounted number of boys worldwide are kidnapped or enticed away from their families or sold by family members to be used in the illegal multimillion-dollar sex industry. One victim, Ny, in Cambodia, was abducted by a local motorbike driver as she was on her way from home to a nearby village to meet her mother. She remembers entering a brothel for the first time. "The girls were all made up, with white powder and red lips," she says, "and I thought men were coming through the door to see a theatrical performance."

That was until the brothel owner led her into a room with a client. Despite Ny's relentless pleading and crying, the brothel owner beat her with electric cables until she could hardly stand. After he left, she was forced to have sex with the client. For the next two years, she was resold from brothel to brothel, enduring beatings and psychological trauma.[15]

Ny was rescued along with more than 200 other girls during a highly publicized 1995 police raid of brothels in one of Cambodia's largest cities. However, such rescues are rare, and child prostitution flourishes in Cambodia with an estimated 20,000 girls and boys forced into the sex industry in that country alone.[16]

Commercial sexual exploitation is one of the most hazardous forms of child labor because of the physical and psychological damages that are inflicted on the victims. It is often accompanied by drug trafficking—kids are forced to sell drugs and/or use them. The children not only risk drug addiction but also have to confront such serious health risks as HIV, the virus that produces AIDS, and girls suffer unwanted pregnancies. In addition, children who are sexually exploited see the world in terms of "distorted reality in which violence and distrust, shame and rejection are the norms." A Senegalese teenager forced into prostitution noted that she and others like her are considered the outcasts of society, and no one wants to be seen with them.[17]

Those who profit from sexual exploitation of children are the agents who procure girls and boys and the criminals who run brothels. Others include business people who arrange tours, primarily for wealthy men traveling to locations where sex with children is available. Those who also gain are creators, publishers, and sellers of pornographic materials and corrupt government officials who are bribed to ignore this type of exploitative child labor. Commercial sexual exploitation of children is not restricted to developing countries. Widespread child prostitution exists in industrialized nations such as the United States, where an estimated 100,000 children are involved in the sex industry.[18] British news reports indicate that in the United Kingdom child prostitutes number between 300,000 and 500,000.[19]

What is being done to stop this type of exploitation? A variety of international organizations—both government and private—are establishing programs to prevent children from being lured or forced into the sex industry. Groups also are pressing for enforcement of local and national laws against this type of sexual abuse and setting up homes and training programs to help victims enter the legitimate workforce and society. Widespread publicity about child prostitution and trafficking is another way that individuals and groups try to induce public pressure to help stop this practice as well as other types of labor hazardous to children.

CHAPTER 4

child WORKERS
IN THE UNITED STATES

Public pressure was one factor that helped bring about changes in child slave-labor practices and the mistreatment of child workers in early American and European factories and mines. The first U.S. factories were textile mills modeled after those that had been operating in Great Britain since the 1770s. Thousands of European and American children worked in textile mills and also at hazardous jobs in coal mines, steel mills, and glass factories. Their experiences were similar to those of child workers in today's developing nations.

A British parliamentary committee conducted interviews in 1832 with young people who had begun work at an early age—frequently at five or six years old—in textile mills, toiling at least fourteen hours per day. The former child workers testified that overseers, or supervisors, scolded and beat children with a strap, especially when they became sleepy and began to doze or were late getting to work. "I generally was beaten when I happened to be too late; and when I got up in the morning the apprehension of that was so great, that I used to run, and cry all the way as I went to the mill," one young man, Matthew Crabtree, testified.[1]

Another former worker, Elizabeth Bentley, said she began working at the age of six as a doffer in a flax mill from six in the morning until seven at night. Elizabeth had to replace full bobbins of thread with empty ones, which required not only dexterity but also speed. If she happened to be slow, she was beaten with a strap. Like others in the mill, she got breakfast when she arrived, but, she reported, the food was "covered with dust; and it was no use to take it home, I could not eat it, and the overlooker [supervisor] took it, and gave it to the pigs."[2]

The bleakness and cruelty of British factory work led one medical expert to note the effects on both adults and children. Their complexion was "sallow and pallid," their limbs were slender with "a general bowing of the legs," and they had "a spiritless and dejected air." Factory labor was not fit for children, who were "cooped up in a heated atmosphere, debarred the necessary exercise, remaining in one position for a series of hours. . . . its effects are injurious to the physical growth of a child."[3]

Because of the parliamentary investigations, in the early 1800s, Britain passed some of the first laws banning child labor, but the laws were seldom enforced. The Factory Act of 1833 banned and helped reduce some of the worst exploitation of children in British textile mills, and U.S. reformers tried—but failed—to pass similar legislation. The British law, however, did not apply to child laborers in iron and coal mines, shipyards, match factories, and other industries. Many of these young workers were in such poor health that they died before they were thirty years old.

U.S. REFORMERS

As the Industrial Revolution spread from Great Britain to the United States during the 1800s and early 1900s, thousands of people migrated to cities and became part of the workforce. Because there were so many workers, there was intense competition for jobs. Workers had to accept low wages, long hours, and hazardous working conditions if they wanted to earn even a meager pay. To survive, many families relied on the small sums that their children earned, which helped perpetuate the cycle of poverty, as is the case today in such countries as Pakistan, India, Bangladesh, Haiti, and the Philippines.

After the Civil War the U.S. factory system expanded, and the production of manufactured goods vastly increased. In the South, for example, the number of cotton textile mills grew from 161 in 1880 to 400 in 1900. Eventually the textile production of the South topped that of New England mills.[4]

Industrialists in the South and the North hired children to work in their factories for the same reasons cited by present-day manufacturers and contractors who use child labor. Early factory owners wanted young workers because they were fast, agile, and easy to control. And there were no pressures to send children to school since education was thought to be of little value for working-class children.

Children, primarily boys, also worked under extremely dangerous conditions in U.S. coal mines in the Appalachian region of the United States. Although fourteen- and fifteen-year-olds could legally work in most mines, many younger boys worked illegally, often as coal breakers. As author Russell Freedman explained in his book *Kids at Work: Lewis Hine and the Crusade Against Child Labor*, the breaker boys worked "outside the mines. Their faces black with soot, they sat in rows on wooden boards placed over coal chutes. As coal came pouring through the chutes, the boys . . . picked out pieces of slate and stone that could not burn. . . . If a boy . . . slipped into the coal that was flowing beneath him, he could be mangled or killed."[5]

When youngsters worked in the mines, their health was threatened by coal dust that filled their lungs and caused chronic respiratory problems. Their health was also impaired because of the long twelve-hour shifts on the job and the exhausting task of stooping and pulling huge baskets or carts of coal out of the mines. Other early industries such as glassmaking employed child workers. Here, too, youngsters were often in grave danger as they worked in furnace rooms, where the heat was intense and the air filled with fumes and dust.

With the dawn of the twentieth century, a period known as the "Progressive Era" began in the United States, and numerous groups and individuals called for economic and social justice for the nation's poor and powerless. Many reform groups fought to establish compulsory education for children. Others agitated for a decent wage, shorter workdays, and better working conditions for laborers.

Conrado Bonilla has been working in the coal mines of Colombia, South America, for three years, since he was thirteen years old. Because his father cannot work, Conrado supports the family with this extremely hard work under conditions similar to those in the United States almost one hundred years ago.

One nonpartisan and broad-based reform group was established in 1904: the National Child Labor Committee (NCLC). A few years later, Congress chartered the NCLC to "promote the welfare of America's working children," and the organization investigated all types of child labor and publicized problems in order to promote state laws that would reduce exploitation of children. From October 1906 to April 1907, the NCLC and several consumer and child-protective organizations conducted a joint investigation of child-labor conditions in New York City tenements. These poorly constructed apartment buildings were crowded, unsafe, and unsanitary. Children living with their families in one or two rooms helped sew clothing or made artificial flowers. In 1908 the NCLC issued a report, noting:

> *In the most thickly populated districts of New York City . . . little children are often seen on the streets carrying large bundles of unfinished garments, or boxes containing materials for making artificial flowers. This work is given out by manufacturers or contractors to be finished in tenement homes, where the labor of children of any age may be utilized. For the laws of New York state, prohibiting the employment of children under fourteen years of age in factories, stores, or other specified work-places, have never been extended to home workrooms.[6]*

The report documented numerous examples of the ways children were employed:

One family made flowers, using the labor of six children, aged two and one-half, five, eight, ten, fourteen and sixteen years. In another family Angelo, aged fourteen years, cannot work legally in a factory until he reaches a higher grade in school, nor can he work at home during hours when school is in session, but his little sister Maria, aged three years, because she is not old enough to go to school and because the home work law contains no prohibition of child labor, may help her mother pull bastings and sew on buttons. . . . Many good citizens would demand the prosecution of a manufacturer who employed in his factory Tony aged four years, Maria aged nine, Rose aged ten, Lousia aged eleven, and Josephine aged thirteen years. . . . Yet the public has not raised an effective protest against the same employer when he turns these children's home into a branch of his factory. . . .[7]

PUBLIC PROTESTS AND CHILD-LABOR LAWS

The public did begin to protest, however, especially after the NCLC report was widely circulated. In addition, the NCLC hired photographer Lewis Hine to document child-labor practices. His haunting pictures clearly and dramatically showed the wretchedness of children working in mills, mines, canneries, and other industries. Some of his dramatic photographs are included in Freedman's book.

Several bills were introduced in the U.S. Congress during the early 1900s to regulate child labor in businesses involved in interstate commerce—selling and transporting goods across state lines. But the NCLC did not support federal legislation. Instead, the organization promoted improved state laws designed to protect children. However, there were very few state inspectors to investigate industries, and even when companies were cited for labor-law violations, the state courts often dismissed cases or levied insignificant fines.[8]

By 1912 the NCLC favored a proposed federal law known as the Palmer-Owen bill, which was sponsored in both the House of Representatives and the Senate. The bill specified that companies engaging in interstate commerce could not hire children under the age of fourteen to work in factories. Children under sixteen were banned from work in mines or quarries. The bill was defeated but eventually passed in 1916 and limited the workday for children under age sixteen to eight hours. Then, in 1918, the U.S. Supreme Court declared the law unconstitutional.

Nevertheless, some of the standards in the act were incorporated into the Fair Labor Standards Act (FLSA) of 1938. It bans child labor in the manufacture of goods that are shipped across state boundaries. The law helped reduce child labor in such industries as mining and manufacturing, but did not cover the employment of children in other types of work. At about the same time, however, states began passing new laws to restrict child labor and to require compulsory education until a specified age (usually sixteen). Labor unions and reform groups also continued their struggles to get child-labor laws enacted in all states.[9]

The FLSA has been amended numerous times and now includes provisions, enforced by a division of the DOL, to protect some of the estimated 5.5 million U.S. youth who are employed. According to the Child Labor Coalition, more than 600,000 of the young workers are illegally employed twelve- and thirteen-year-olds whose wages are "paid under the table." The total does not include children as young as six, seven, or eight years of age who work in agriculture.

Requirements cover child labor according to age groups and types of occupations. Work hours for minors are also regulated. When school is in session, minors are limited to three hours of work per school day and eight hours on non-school days. Work hours are restricted to the period from 7:00 A.M. to 7:00 P.M. However, from June 1 through Labor Day, the workday can extend to 9:00 P.M.

In nonagricultural occupations, minors under the age of eighteen are banned from jobs that are declared hazardous by the U.S. secretary of labor. These include any type of mining, logging, and saw milling, working with explosives and radioactive materials, brick manufacturing, excavation, operating power-driven machinery, and slaughtering and meatpacking. There are exceptions for sixteen- and seventeen-year-olds who are in apprentice or vocational education programs. Those aged fourteen and fifteen may work a limited number of hours beyond the school day in nonhazardous jobs. At any age, children are allowed to deliver newspapers; perform in stage productions, movies, radio and television shows; and work in a business solely owned by their parents.

Workers involved in the production of agricultural goods that directly or indirectly leave the state and become a part of interstate commerce also are covered to some extent by the FLSA. Young people sixteen years of age and over may work in any farm job at any time. Children ten and eleven years old may be employed outside school hours under prescribed conditions to harvest short-season crops by hand for no more than eight weeks, between June 1 and October 15 in any calendar year. Minors of any age may work at any time in any job on a farm owned or operated by their parents, the DOL states.[10]

Today, laws and regulations in every state govern the employment of minors, but these can vary by state and may differ from federal regulations. If a state law is more stringent than the federal standards, the state law must be observed. For example, the FLSA does not require minors to obtain a work permit in order to be employed, but in many states a minor must get a "permit to employ" from the state department of labor or employment. An employer is required to keep the permit on file for as long as the minor is employed. To cite another difference: the FLSA does not limit either the number of hours nor the time of day that youths sixteen years of age and older may work; but some state laws do restrict work hours for sixteen- and seventeen-year-olds. The state law, then, overrides the federal law.

CHILD-LABOR VIOLATIONS

Most business people try to abide by federal and state laws designed to protect children from work that damages their health and well-being or interferes with their education. Yet "the United States ranks first among affluent nations in the rate of injury and death to working minors," noted U.S. Representative Tom Lantos of California in a speech before the House of Representatives. "Annually there are over 200,000 injuries of children and young people in our Nation's workplaces and 100 deaths among our working youth. In agriculture, 23,500 children are injured each year and more than 300 children die each year working in the fields."

Lantos also pointed out that "sweatshops have returned in the United States in numbers and forms that are similar to the deplorable conditions that existed at the turn of the century." He cited an example of young immigrant women, some of them teenagers, from Thailand and Mexico who were discovered in 1995 inside a California compound surrounded by a high wall and barbed wire. They were forced to work twenty hours per day making clothing in deplorable conditions for as little as $1 per hour. (In 1997 the Asian Pacific American Legal Center won a law suit on the workers' behalf, and five companies who contracted with the sweatshop owners agreed to pay the workers $2 million.) The General Accounting Office "recently reported that 2,000 of 6,000 garment shops in New York City and most of the 5,000 shops in Los Angeles operate in violation of minimum wage, overtime, or child-labor laws," Lantos told House members.[11]

During the last five months of 1997, reporters for the Associated Press (AP) investigated various workplaces in sixteen states and "found 165 children working illegally." Some were only four years old working in agricultural fields; others were teenagers such as Vielesee Cassell, 13, who spent the summer folding and bagging dresses in a Texas sweatshop.[12]

The Associated Press also hired Douglas Kruse, a Rutgers University economist, to analyze government data and estimate the number of children employed illegally in the United States. In his study, Kruse concluded that "290,000 children were employed unlawfully" in 1996. Among them were "13,100 who worked in garment sweatshops, defined as factories with repeated labor violations." In addition his study showed that employers who hired underage rather than legal workers "saved $155 million in wages" during 1996.[13]

Some of the most frequent violations of U.S. child-labor laws have occurred in restaurants, according to a study published in *Cornell Hotel & Restaurant Administration Quarterly*.[14] Although such businesses—especially fast-food chains—provide numerous entry-level jobs for teenagers, company managers may ignore or be ignorant of federal and state child-labor laws. For example, restaurants may be fined for allowing teenagers to make deliveries or to work with meat slicers and perform other jobs deemed too hazardous for youths under eighteen. Most infractions, though, involve the number of hours and time periods that minors work.

Each minor in violation of a child-labor regulation can cost an employer up to $10,000. For example, the DOL fined Burger King at least $500,000 in 1991 for not complying with various child-labor regulations. A few years later, a fine of $10,500 was levied against a restaurant chain in Minneapolis, Minnesota, because teenagers younger than sixteen worked more hours than legally allowed.[15] Early in 1997, the Golden Corral restaurant in St. Charles, Missouri, was fined $6,750 for allowing "at least 10 minors to work until 12:30 A.M. and more than seven hours on school days. . . . On weekends, the minors were working more than nine hours a day," the *St. Louis Post-Dispatch* reported.[16]

Such violations of child-labor regulations have also occurred in supermarkets and businesses like car washes, gas stations, and other service industries where young people are commonly employed. Agriculture, however, may be the industry in which child-labor compliance is the most lax, in spite of the fact that fewer regulations protect farmworkers. In fact, about half of the states have no minimum age for agricultural laborers, and many states extend the hours children can work while school is in session, or set no maximum at all. According to the Child Labor Coalition "57 percent of the states do not set maximum hours for fourteen- and fifteen-year-olds and 78 percent do not set maximum hours for sixteen- and seventeen-year-olds."[17]

In their five-month investigation of child labor, AP's reporters found "104 children working illegally in agriculture . . . nearly three times the 35 that U.S. Labor Department inspectors witnessed nationwide" in 1996. As the AP report explained, "Underage children picked cucumbers in Michigan, green peppers in Tennessee, and apples in upstate New York. Their grape-cutting knives flashed in the sunny vineyards of California, and their headlamps bobbed in the gloomy mushroom sheds of Pennsylvania. They packed peaches into crates in Illinois and hoed sorghum in Lubbock, Texas."[18]

HAZARDS OF FARMWORK

According to many child-welfare advocates as well as labor leaders, agricultural work is one of the most dangerous occupations in the United States and is especially hazardous for young child workers. The FLSA bans minors under sixteen from working at hazardous farm jobs, which include operating or assisting anyone operating such machinery as a corn or cotton picker, grain combine, hay mower, and various other equipment. That ban, however, does not apply to children who work on family-owned farms.

In one tragic incident, a twelve-year-old boy, like many children who live on farms, was allowed to work in his family's fields. He was walking alongside a hay mower "when his shirttail got tangled in the machine. Screaming and struggling to free himself, he was yanked off his feet and under the whirling blades." His screams were drowned out by the sounds of the farm machinery and by the time the driver stopped it was too late to save the boy.[19]

Jacob was another victim of such hazards. When he was five years old he worked with his migrant family as they moved from state to state picking and sorting fruits and vegetables. While his family was in Tifton, Georgia, Jacob helped sort watermelons and package them for shipment. His arm and hand were caught in a conveyor

Alejandra Renteria is six years old and has been working in the fields alongside her sister and parents long
enough to have a preference—she says she'd rather be
picking fruit in her home state of Florida than doing
the backbreaking work of picking cucumbers in this
field in Ohio.

belt and ripped off. Although doctors were able to reattach his arm, they were unable to save his hand.[20]

Migrant child workers, estimated at 800,000 in the United States, are particularly vulnerable to farm hazards. Like Jacob, youngsters often work illegally in the fields. They are not registered as workers, but they may be part of a work crew organized by a contractor who supplies laborers for growers. The laborers may be entire families who are employed under one social security number—a head of household who receives and distributes the wages. Because affordable day care is not readily available for many migrant families, very young children may accompany their parents to the fields and play nearby while their parents work. In Florida, where many migrant families work, one observer said that she often saw young children out in the fields, and one year a child "was run over in the field by a tractor. Another year two kids drowned. They were playing in some ditches . . . while their parents worked."[21]

Migrant children working or accompanying their parents in fields also risk pesticide poisoning. Children may pick crops that are still wet with pesticide sprays, or may themselves apply pesticides on plants. Young children are more sensitive than adults to poisonous chemicals, and exposure to toxins can lead to ailments such as skin and eye irritations, respiratory and neurological problems, according to scientists and public-health experts.

A MODEL LAW

To combat the hazards posed for children who are migrant or seasonal workers, the Child Labor Coalition is encouraging states to set a minimum age of fourteen for employment in agriculture and to regulate work hours for minor farmworkers in the same way it does for child workers in other types of jobs. The CLC included these recommendations in a Model State Child Labor Law, which was developed after a year of research and has been presented since the early 1990s to states that are attempting to amend their child-labor regulations.

Among other provisions in the Model Law, the CLC suggests a permit system that "requires the involvement of parents, educators, and employers in the minor's educational and work experience." To obtain a permit, a minor would be required to show legal proof of age along with his or her name and address. Additional specific requirements would include the:

- employer's name, address, signature, and description of employment
- parent or legal guardian's signature approving employment as in the best interest of the minor
- signature of school official or teaching professional, knowledgeable about state child labor law and academic performance of the minor, approving employment as in the best interest of the minor[22]

The Model Law also includes provisions to more vigorously prosecute employers who violate child-labor regulations. Information about violators should be widely distributed to students, parents, and employers, the CLC maintains.

CHAPTER 5

HOW GLOBAL
COMPANIES EXPLOIT
children

As American corporations and other companies based in highly industrial nations have become global in scope, less industrialized nations compete for foreign investment by offering low-cost labor and production facilities. This usually means that children will be involved in production. For example, vegetable growers such as Bosocovich Farms, Muranaka Farms, Fresh Choice, and Phoenix Vegetable Growers have moved some if not most of their operations to Mexico. There child labor is illegal but is not strictly regulated, especially in agriculture. "Companies achieve greater competitiveness at the cost of children working in the fields," according to David Bacon of the Pacific News Service. He reported that in the Mexican countryside just south of the Mexico-U.S. border, child labor is cutting into school attendance even as the school-age population grows. Some rural schools in the Mexicali Valley have been closed down for lack of students.

Gema Lopez Limon, a researcher from the University of Baja California, described farm laboring crews in the valley made up of entire families. Piece rates are so low for harvesting green onions and tomatoes that the income of the parents alone can no longer feed the family.[1]

Large U.S. food-producing companies, known as agribusinesses, are not the only ones who gain from the low-paid labor of children. Since the early 1990s, the U.S. apparel industry has been under attack because of numerous reports about the use and abuse of child labor in overseas factories producing clothing for export to the United States. In addition, there has been mounting public criticism of American-based companies that use overseas contractors employing child workers to produce sporting goods, toys, and carpets for export to the United States and Canada.

SWEATSHOPS IN BANGLADESH AND OTHER COUNTRIES

In 1993 an NBC *Dateline* television program showed children in Bangladesh working in sweatshops to make clothing for Wal-Mart stores. As a result, Wal-Mart canceled its contracts with Bangladeshi garment makers, as did several other U.S.-based companies. The Bangladesh Garment Manufacturers and Exporters Association (BGMEA), which represents an industry that employs more than one million workers, feared the loss of its lucrative exports to the United States. Tens of thousands of children were dismissed from garment factories. Apparently, this forced some minors to work in underground, or secret, shops with worse conditions than the factories they had left. Or they found work in hazardous jobs such as stone-crushing and brickmaking. Some became domestic servants or ended up in prostitution.[2] When representatives of international organizations and officials of the U.S. Embassy learned about the situation, they asked the BGMEA to stop firing underage workers until there were better options for the dismissed children. After difficult and extended negotiations the BGMEA, the ILO, and UNICEF created and signed a Memorandum of Understanding (MOU) in 1995. The three organizations provide funds to implement the MOU, which has four key provisions:

1. Remove all underage workers from garment factories and enroll them in schools.
2. Forbid hiring of underage workers, as well as any retention of children once all schools have opened.
3. Provide a monthly stipend (equivalent to about $7.00) for families who depended on the income of former child workers.
4. Offer employment to adult family members of underage workers whose employment is terminated.[3]

In its first international report in 1994 (*By the Sweat and Toil of Children*, Volume I), the DOL's Bureau of International Labor Affairs gathered information on underage garment workers not only in Bangladesh but also in Brazil, China, Guatemala, India, Indonesia, Lesotho, Morocco, the Philippines, Portugal, and Thailand. Although the report noted that "more research was necessary to confirm the extent and working conditions of child workers," in these countries there was evidence that "children were involved in the production of garments for export to the United States." Children were likely to work in small subcontracting shops or home work situations. In some cases, children were found to work in locked shops, with armed guards preventing entrance and exit during work hours. Children worked on tasks such as sewing buttons, cutting and trimming threads, folding, moving and packing garments. In small shops and homesites in the Philippines, children were also found embroidering and smocking (making pleats). In some cases, children worked long hours sometimes six or seven days a week. Some children received less than the minimum wage and were not paid for overtime work.[4]

Two years after the initial investigation, there was little doubt that minors were still working in the garment industry in a number of countries, although no exact totals were (or are) available because of the way U.S.-based companies subcontract work to a network of overseas operations. However, there are indications that the number of children working on garment exports for the U.S. market may be declining, according to the 1996 ILAB report. Yet officials caution that they have gathered only anecdotal evidence in six countries: the Dominican Republic, El Salvador, Guatemala, Honduras, India, and the Philippines. Officials say "more research is necessary to confirm that a downward trend in the use of child labor in garment production is a universal phenomenon. This is no small task since a total of 168 countries export apparel to the U.S. market, many of them small suppliers."[5]

SPOTLIGHT ON U.S.-BASED GARMENT AND FOOTWEAR COMPANIES

Despite international investigations, child-labor abuses in the apparel industry did not draw widespread media attention until the spotlight fell on overseas sweatshops making clothing with celebrity labels. Information about such sweatshops was revealed in April 1996 when Charles Kernaghan, executive director of the National Labor Committee, a human-rights group, testified before a congressional committee looking into labor abuses. Kernaghan described complaints he had received from fifteen-year-old Wendy Diaz of Honduras. Diaz had been employed in Honduras at Global Fashions, a Korean-owned company that makes clothing for export. At the time, Global Fashions made a line of pants bearing the label of Kathie Lee Gifford, a popular talk-show host.

Diaz was one of the child workers making this line of clothing. She began working at the factory when she was thirteen years old, and claimed that her employers exploited child workers, forcing them to work up to 20 hours per day in extreme heat for 31 cents an hour. They were also subjected to physical and verbal abuse and were not allowed to speak, Diaz charged. Workers who tried to organize a labor union for protection were fired.

Wal-Mart stores, which sells the Gifford clothing, at first vigorously denied the charges, and Gifford was indignant that anyone would imply that she did not care about children. She angrily told reporters, "I started my clothing line to benefit children. Millions of dollars have gone to help children, and I truly resent this man [Kernaghan] impugning my integrity."[6] Not long after-

Kathie Lee Gifford calls on the clothing industry to police itself and stop using child labor in factories abroad.

ward Gifford acknowledged that sweatshop conditions did exist in the factory making her clothing line and that all ties had been cut with the Global Fashion plant in Honduras. Wal-Mart also canceled orders with factories making other products under sweatshop conditions.

Gifford began a crusade to try to eliminate sweatshops in the apparel industry—whether overseas or in the United States—and called attention to other companies and celebrity lines (such as Walt Disney clothes and Nike shoes with Michael Jordan's label). As a result, much media attention has focused on the issue of overseas sweatshops and child labor in the production of goods exported to the United States. In addition, congressional leaders and child-welfare advocates have called for other celebrities to follow Gifford's example. Michael Jordan, for example, became a target because Nike pays him millions of dollars to endorse a line of footwear that some critics say are made under sweatshoplike conditions. Like most other global companies, Nike owns no factories overseas. It contracts with some 300 manufacturers in 32 countries, although many of the manufacturing plants in Asia are owned by only a few families. Some labor activists claim they have seen ten-year-old children working in factories where Nike shoes are made.

Critics contend that Jordan should at least speak out about labor abuses. When Jordan was asked in 1996 whether Nike exploits workers, he told a *Time* magazine reporter, "I'm not really aware of that. My job with Nike is to endorse the product. Their job is to be up on that."[7]

Jordan's comment did little to satisfy labor and child-welfare activists, and some have called for a boycott of

Nike products. Nike officials, on the other hand, have consistently defended their company's policies and practices. Spokesman Dusty Kidd, Nike's director of labor practices, pointed out that through its contractors, Nike provides between 300,000 and 500,000 jobs overseas. About 30 percent of those jobs are the result of high retail sales of products with the Jordan label. Although overseas workers earn much less than Americans do, Kidd insists that Nike abides by the legal minimum wage established by various countries and also monitors its overseas factories for labor, health, and safety violations.[8]

Other companies, such as the Gap, Liz Claiborne, Levi Strauss, Reebok, and Eddie Bauer have also been under fire for contracting with firms that exploit workers, although not all have been accused of using child labor. Some of these companies, however, have taken action in response to public criticism. The Gap and Levi's are regularly held up as examples of corporations that have required their suppliers to comply with labor laws.

Until recent years, however, few officials in U.S. corporations or members of the general public had given much thought to the welfare of those making the products that American-based companies sell. Congressional committees held hearings on this issue in the 1990s, but the news media hardly covered the proceedings. It was only after Gifford testified that cameras appeared and news coverage was assured. As a result, an increasing number of companies began to feel pressure from consumers, human-rights activists, and government officials to monitor plants that export products to the United States and Canada.

Nevertheless, as Gifford discovered, "there is no one overnight solution to the problem" of labor abuses. Testifying before a House Subcommittee on International Organizations and Human Rights in July 1996, Gifford told congressional members:

> . . . we are beginning to create a framework for solutions. For starters, working with Wal-Mart, I plan to implement a plan whereby any Kathie Lee fashion wear will be done in factories willing to submit to surprise inspections by an independent inspector-general team. Their mission will be to ensure that safe and responsible working conditions are met. Factories that refuse inspection, or ignore warnings, will be dropped as manufacturers.
>
> And yet taking work out of factories that abuse their employees puts those employees on unemployment. . . . Ironically, the factory in Honduras where Wendy Diaz was abused continues to employ a steady 1,000 people even after Wal-Mart pulled their work that carries my name. . . . Punitive actions don't seem to phase the owners of this particular factory.[9]

MAKING SOCCER BALLS IN SWEATSHOPS

About the time that garment makers came under attack, abuses in the soccer-ball industry were being publicized worldwide in news reports and TV documentaries. For example, in his major feature for *Life* magazine, Sydney

Schanberg reported on his visit to Pakistan, where 75 to 80 percent of the world's soccer balls are produced for such global companies as Adidas, Brine, Nike, Reebok, and Umbro. (Pakistan is also notorious for forcing bonded and enslaved children such as Iqbal Masih to make carpets for export to affluent countries.) The United States imports 9 million soccer balls each year from Pakistan.

During his visit, Schanberg went to Sialkot, "the hub of the nation's soccer ball industry, producing about 35 million balls a year." Adult factory workers in Sialkot cut the leather pieces for the soccer balls and put these and other parts into kits, which are then sent to villages nearby where children—many of them bonded workers—stitch the balls together. According to Schanberg:

> Stitching sheds are visible in every hamlet, but at each stop the masters shout at the boys to run when they see foreigners with cameras. And the ragged, barefoot kids, fearing a beating from their masters, dash into the thickets and rice fields beyond. At one compound that resembles a nest of grungy one-car garages, with no lights or ventilation, the soccer masters run shed to shed, yelling at the children to strip off the rubber finger-wraps designed to protect them from disabling thread cuts and to flee for cover.[10]

Child laborers earn the equivalent of 6 cents an hour stitching soccer balls. If they are bonded workers, their earnings are applied to the debt incurred by their parents or other relatives, which literally makes them enslaved until the loan is repaid.

Some changes are under way, however. In 1994, when Reebok got into the soccer-ball industry in Sialkot, the company built a modern factory where all production takes place and the minimum age for workers is fifteen. To make sure that materials are not smuggled out of the factory to clandestine child workers, Reebok has hired local activists to make inspections in nearby villages. Auditors also check the production line to count the number of finished balls that will be shipped from the factory.

In 1997, Reebok asked Olympic gold medalist Julie Foudy to endorse a soccer ball made in Pakistan. Foudy, who was aware of the child-labor problems in the industry, would not allow her name to be used until she visited the Sialkot factory to see the conditions for herself. After her visit in March, she was convinced that the Reebok plant was abiding by international labor standards and that products were made by adults only. She agreed to be a sponsor, but she said she could "never look at a ball the same way again" because of the intensive hand labor involved in its manufacture.

According to a news report, "The stitchers Foudy saw . . . spend their days on low wooden benches, looping the thread between the big and first toes of one foot so that it functions as a bobin, painstakingly puncturing the leather panels with an awl and drawing the thread through." Sewing the 32 leather panels of a ball together requires 642 stitches, and skilled stitchers can complete only three or four balls per day, earning an equivalent of about $2.25 plus benefits, which is considered a high wage in Pakistan. In Foudy's view, athletes should take an active role in helping to ensure that products are not made with child labor. She acknowledged that most athletes "don't want to be bothered with the questions. But they're in the public eye, and they can draw attention to the problems."[11]

Whether or not athletes are involved in this issue, numerous grassroots groups, including many student groups, and government and trade organizations, are actively pursuing changes. Thousands of students across North America and Europe, for example, have taken part in the FoulBall Campaign, a program of the International Labor Rights Fund. It was initiated in 1996 to pressure the Federation of International Football Associations (FIFA) based in Zurich, Switzerland, to withhold endorsement of soccer balls made by exploited children. Students wrote letters protesting the use of such sporting goods, and by the end of the year association officials agreed to withhold FIFA's seal of approval from companies that do not meet independent inspection standards prohibiting child labor in factories.

In February 1997, a coalition that includes the ILO and some fifty manufacturers—Adidas, Reebok, and Nike among them—and Pakistani industrialists, signed an agreement to eliminate child labor in Pakistan's soccer-ball industry within eighteen months. In November 1997, fifteen independent monitors representing the coalition began monthly inspections of 140 centers where soccer balls are stitched. These centers were set up to replace some of the stitching sheds in villages, thus making it easier to monitor working conditions.

"To ensure that children aren't stitching, Pakistani manufacturers who supply the balls to U.S. companies must name their stitchers and account for production from each center," according to the Associated Press.

What happens to the children who can no longer work? UNICEF has pledged $200,000 to "improve school equipment and train teachers so that the children who had been working—and others who might try to—can go to school instead." A Pakistani bank, backed by the nation's government, is making credit available so that local organizations can help families find income other than that earned by their children's labor. In addition, the U.S. government has provided $750,000 for the coalition's work, the AP reported.[12]

Because the soccer-ball industry is concentrated in Sialkot, there are high hopes that child labor can be eliminated in the region. But the industry could spread to other areas of Pakistan or to other countries where child labor is not as visible. No one expects that exploitation of children in sporting goods or other industries will be solved quickly, but the monitoring coalition at least is one example of an international effort to share responsibility and address a major world problem.

CHAPTER 6

WHO'S
RESPONSIBLE?

Even as activists try to prevent American-based multinational companies from using subcontractors who employ children, some business advocates argue that long hours in garment factories and tedious work in Pakistani "stitching sheds" are better than no paid work at all. In fact, in 1996, David R. Henderson in *Fortune* magazine criticized Secretary of Labor Robert Reich and groups such as the National Labor Committee for trying to make consumers believe that sweatshops are unethical. In his view, labor groups try "to intimidate American companies and consumers who wish to buy goods made with low-wage labor." Henderson contended that even though "a low-paying job in Honduras or in the Los Angeles garment district seems horrible . . . for many adults and children, it's the best choice they have. You don't make someone better off by taking away the best of her bad options." Henderson claimed that consumers should not "feel guilty for buying clothing made in Honduras, Viet-nam, or Bangladesh." Why? Because, he writes, "You're helping the workers who made it—and who were unlucky enough to have been born in a poor country. The people who should feel guilty are . . . [those] who push policies that hurt the very people they claim to care about."[1]

Such an argument was often used by opponents of child-labor reforms and organized-labor efforts during the Industrial Revolution. Many critics of early reform movements in the United States condemned proposed laws that would protect workers, calling it government interference. That contention is the basis for the view of one of today's critics, Llewellyn Rockwell, Jr. Writing for *Insight on the News*, Rockwell declared that labor unions are the primary force behind efforts to ban children from workforces in poor countries because children compete with union labor for jobs. As he put it:

> *Labor protectionists can dream up endless stories of tiny babes slaving dawn to dusk. . . . We have no way to assess the truth of these tales, and the wise listener will consider the source. For workers to be valuable to employers, after all, they must be able to produce valuable work. If they are of an age to do so, who is to say that governments should intervene to prevent it?*[2]

Rockwell argues that in affluent industrial societies, parents can "delay the entry of their children into the workforce for many years," but that "option is not available in poor countries," which many child-welfare advo-

cates have pointed out as well. "Child labor is a necessary part of economic development," Rockwell writes,
adding that putting children "to work in their early teens
. . . allows families undergoing extreme hardship to support themselves. Children contribute to family income
and gain valuable experience and are seen as a net asset
to families and society."[3]

An editorial in the *Houston Chronicle* partially agrees
that even though working conditions in sweatshops may
be terrible, "they are often the only jobs available to the
local people. It is not unusual for the sweatshop operations to pay more money and provide more benefits than
the local people can find elsewhere. For them, work in
the sweatshops, even that almost akin to slave labor, is
seen as a better life." However the editorial writer argues that "hugely profitable companies . . . have a moral
obligation to deal with their workers fairly. When, for
example, billion-dollar footwear manufacturers produce
sport shoes for a couple of dollars and sell them for $200,
while paying their workers barely enough to survive, they
deserve whatever criticism they receive."[4]

BEING ACCOUNTABLE

An increasing number of consumers are voicing opin-
ions on who should be held accountable for sweatshops.
In one survey conducted in 1996 by the International
Mass Retail Association (IMRA), nearly 33 percent of
1,000 consumers polled thought that U.S. companies
making products in other nations should be "responsible
for controlling abusive labor practices," and 18 percent
thought retailers should assume that obligation. How-

ever, 46 percent "reported that foreign and domestic government had the main responsibility to police exploitative labor practices in foreign countries."[5]

Along with consumer groups, numerous religious, environmental, and labor organizations have called for governments as well as American global corporations to be morally and socially responsible in international trade dealings. Activists say that because a giant corporation exerts great economic influence, it has political clout in some countries and could (and should) take a stand against inhumane, unjust, and criminal actions of their subsidiaries, including in particular illegal child-labor practices.

On October 4, 1997, groups across North America and around the world took part in a National Day of Conscience, initiating a three-month Holiday Shopping Season of Conscience. It was part of what supporters called a national and international movement to encourage consumers to buy from companies that eliminate sweatshops and labor exploitation and penalize those that continue to violate human rights. Rallies, vigils, candlelight marches, interdenominational services, street theater, and many other activities during the holiday season were designed to urge retailers to be aware of how goods are made—especially clothing—and to be responsible for what they sell.

CODES OF CONDUCT AND LABELING PROGRAMS

As diverse groups have increasingly urged companies to take responsibility for the conditions under which their

These students from New York City were among many that participated in a National Day of Conscience. Media coverage of the event successfully put child-labor issues in the news again, raising the awareness level yet another notch.

goods are being manufactured, corporate codes of conduct and other business policies that prohibit the use of child labor have become more common. Corporate codes of conduct stem from guidelines that various global companies and voluntary groups developed beginning in the 1970s. One of the first such codes was presented by the Reverend Leon Sullivan, a black clergyman in the United States, who hoped to help end apartheid (legal separation of groups according to color codes) in South Africa by regulating U.S.-based corporations operating there. Although the Sullivan principles, as the codes are known, did little to end apartheid, "they did alter the conduct of some U.S. firms, at least with regard to the most blatant forms of racial discrimination in the workplace," according to legal expert Christine Elwell of Queens University in Kingston, Ontario, Canada.[6]

Other voluntary guidelines for global companies were established by United Nations agencies, nongovernmental organizations, and trade-union committees during the 1970s and 1980s. One such group, founded in 1989, is the Coalition (formerly the Committee) for Justice in the Maquiladoras (CJM). *Maquiladoras* is a term for the several thousand factories located in a region just south of the Mexico–United States border. American corporations (as well as those of other industrialized nations) have set up industries in this zone, where Mexican workers assemble products. The goods are then sent to twin plants, or *maquilas*, in the United States, where they are packaged for sale. But the *maquiladora* system operates in Mexico without the environmental, health, and safety standards imposed in the United States. Mexican workers also earn much less than U.S. workers.

The CJM, which is composed of representatives from religious and environmental groups, trade unions, and others, issued a proposed code of conduct for the *maquiladoras* and mounted a public campaign to press for U.S. companies to abide by standards of conduct that are based on American and Mexican laws. These standards would help assure healthy and safe workplaces, eliminate toxic chemicals that pollute factories and the environment, and establish a decent wage for workers.

In 1991 the apparel industry began to set codes of conduct, including provisions banning child labor, but the practice did not become widespread until after Kathie Lee Gifford helped make sweatshops an issue nationwide, if not worldwide, in 1995. Following the recommendations of Secretary of Labor Robert Reich, who campaigned throughout his tenure for an end to labor abuses, President Bill Clinton convened an Apparel Industry Partnership task force in mid-1996 to help eliminate sweatshops in the apparel industry. The task force includes members of human-rights groups, representatives of such firms as Nike, Reebok, Liz Claiborne, Patagonia, and L.L. Bean, and leaders of two labor unions, Union of Needletrades, Industrial and Textile Employees (UNITE) and the Retail, Wholesale and Department Store Union.

In April 1997, after eight months of intense negotiations with DOL and other federal government officials, the task force reached an agreement on an industry code, which the group hopes will be voluntarily used by apparel manufacturers. The code prohibits employment of children—those younger than fifteen, except in countries that allow fourteen-year-olds to work. It also recognizes workers' right to organize, bargain, and work in a healthy and safe environment; sets a maximum work-week of sixty hours; and requires companies to pay at least the minimum wage established in the nations where they operate. Companies that abide by the code will be certified to use a "no sweat" label or other type of tag stating that their apparel was not manufactured in sweat-shops.

The no-sweat label would be similar to labeling programs already in effect for other U.S. imports. The FoulBall label, as described previously, is applied to FIFA-approved soccer balls that are child-labor free. Another is the RUGMARK label. Because of the widespread publicity about bonded children in the carpet industries of such countries as Pakistan, India, and Nepal, rugs made without child labor are tagged with a RUGMARK logo bearing a child's smiling face. The RUGMARK Foundation certifies companies that qualify for the logo and routinely inspects carpet makers to ensure that the certification is valid. These rugs are exported primarily to North America, Europe, and Japan. Importers pay one percent of the value of the rug to the RUGMARK Foundation, which uses the tax to pay for schools and educational projects in carpet-producing countries.

Both the RUGMARK and FoulBall labeling programs are only beginning efforts to eliminate child labor in specific industries. Establishing a no-sweat code (and label) for the apparel industry is also only a first step. An even more difficult process is monitoring to determine whether companies can legitimately use the no-sweat label. Some apparel manufacturers oppose any type of monitoring of their facilities, arguing that such a tag could be counterfeited. Human-rights activists, nongovern-mental organizations, and union leaders insist that a labeling program will not work unless independent monitors can ensure that all the manufacturers are in compliance.

Some companies hire private firms to monitor their overseas operations, but these monitors are accountable only to those who employ them. This has been the case with high-profile companies like Nike and Disney. In 1997, Nike hired former UN Ambassador Andrew Young to investigate and report on some of the company's sub-contractors and monitors in Asia. Young found that al-though independent auditors checked Nike factories for compliance and managers understood the company's code of conduct, workers did not. Thus, at Young's rec-ommendation, Nike issued wallet-size code-of-conduct cards in the native languages of its workers and manag-ers. According to a Nike press release, more than 100,000 Nike footwear contract factory workers in Asia were among the first to receive the cards in the fall of 1997. "The dual-sided, laminated cards . . . inform workers of their rights and benefits in the areas of health, safety, compensation and wages."[7]

Nevertheless, some independent observers have not given Nike high marks for its efforts. American business-man Thuyen Nguyen also investigated Nike's factories in 1997 and issued a report stating that workers in Viet-nam earned the U.S. equivalent of 20 cents an hour. They were "forced into overtime and subjected to extreme corporal punishment, including having their mouths taped shut for stepping out of line and being forced to run in circles in the sweltering sun."[8]

Public pressure and media criticism, however, are having an effect on numerous companies. It is not unusual today for businesses to announce that they have set up programs to label or certify their products as child-labor free. In early 1998, for example, the Gem River company, which mines sapphires in western Montana, issued a press release to assure its customers and retailers that the company did not hire children to polish its gems. Many of the sapphires are sent to contractors overseas for cutting and polishing. According to the company's president, Tom Lee, "Gem River has always maintained a policy of refusing to use child labor, either directly or indirectly, through contractors in other countries," but, he added, "we have recently begun to receive inquiries about this issue from retail jewelers. Therefore, we concluded it was an appropriate time to issue a certificate attesting to a policy we have maintained since the inception of our company."[9]

A SOCIAL STANDARD

Besides certification programs and corporate codes of conduct, numerous organizations and some global corporations are pressuring for a so-called social clause or social standard in international trade agreements. Representatives of various groups announced in late 1997 that they support a standard known as Social Accountability 8000 (SA8000), which was initiated by the Council on Economic Priorities Accreditation Agency (CEPAA). The council's advisory board includes representatives of such corporations as Avon Products, The Body Shop, Toys R Us, Eileen Fisher, Inc., and other global companies based in European and Latin American countries. NGO

(Non-Governmental Organizations) members of the board include Amnesty International, the National Child Labor Committee, and the University of Texas.[10]

Pointing out the need for the universal standard, the CEPAA notes that "factory managers are deluged with a great number of inconsistent standards and terminologies as companies, NGOs and governments individually present their solutions to the problems of child labor, forced labor, discrimination, workplace conditions, etc." According to Alice Tepper Marlin, president of CEPAA, the standards will provide a means by which "companies and consumers can accurately know the policy and the practices of the companies whose goods they purchase." But setting social standards, like establishing corporate codes of conduct, is only a small part of the process. A larger and more difficult task is enforcing provisions for "reliable" and "truly independent" audits of corporate operations in developing nations.[11]

The concept of an accountability standard has been highly controversial, however. Government officials in some Asian and Latin American countries claim that it is a form of protectionism for industrialized nations. A universal standard, opponents say, would place developing countries at a disadvantage because offering low-wage labor is one way that a poor country can compete with a rich country in international trade.

FEDERAL, STATE, AND LOCAL LAWS

During the early 1990s, Senator Tom Harkin of Iowa proposed a federal law that calls for a ban on the commercial exploitation of children and prohibits the import of products made by child labor. Harkin's proposed bill would require the secretary of labor to identify foreign industries that use child labor. Companies violating the prohibition against importing these products would be subject to stiff penalties.

Over several years the proposed law, now known as the Child Labor Deterrence Act, has been reintroduced along with a companion bill in the House. In 1994 a total of 112 Nobel laureates announced their support for the measure and established the Childright Worldwide Organization, which links legislative and nonlegislative initiatives to end child exploitation. However, no vote has been taken on either the Senate or House bill, and both proposals were still pending at the beginning of 1998.

Some states have passed legislation to eliminate labor exploitation, especially in domestic sweatshops. Legislators in New Jersey, which has an estimated 200 sweatshops making apparel, enacted a stringent anti-sweatshop law in 1996. According to a report in *Women's Wear Daily* the law allows the state to confiscate "equipment and unfinished and finished goods . . . if manufacturers commit three labor violations within three years." Violations include noncompliance with child-labor laws as well as laws governing wages, work hours, and unemployment.[12]

A similar law was passed in California, but that legislation requires a court order to confiscate goods and equipment of violators, which is not the case in New Jersey. Under New Jersey law, "the state takes control of the merchandise and must ensure it does not enter the stream of commerce. It would likely be donated to a state hospital or the like," New Jersey's labor commissioner explained.[13]

Some U.S. cities are also passing laws to ensure that the goods they purchase are not made in foreign or domestic sweatshops. In February 1997, North Olmsted, Ohio, made labor history when "it became the first U.S. municipality to adopt an official policy barring the purchase of goods produced in sweatshops," according to *Women's Wear Daily*. The city council passed a resolution that "prohibits the city from purchasing, renting or leasing uniforms" or such items as sports equipment for the city's recreation department that "have been manufactured under sweatshop conditions and/or through the exploitation of workers and/or the abuse of child labor." The labor union UNITE provided guidelines for enforcing the city policy and is hopeful that North Olmsted's resolution will be a model for other U.S. cities.[14]

Although it is too early to tell whether a trend is under way to enact sweatshop resolutions and laws in other cities, some have followed North Olmsted's example. In June 1997, San Francisco enacted an ordinance banning goods produced in sweatshops, and such cities as Cleveland, Ohio; Philadelphia, Pennsylvania; Bangor, Maine; and New York City are considering or have passed similar legislation.

THE "BOTTOM LINE"

Federal, state, and local laws in the United States and codes of conduct initiated by U.S. global corporations can help stem the flow of goods produced by exploited children. But these actions are of little value if developing nations do not enforce child-labor legislation, particularly laws that set a minimum age for entering employment. Families also need a means to earn income other than that provided by their children, so a nation's economic growth and development are of major importance in eliminating child labor. Basic social services, such as primary education, health care, and food subsidies for the poor, are other notable factors.

In short, putting an end to child labor requires changes on many fronts, especially in attitudes about child labor and the world's poor. To help bring about changes in attitudes, activists in many countries are raising awareness that child labor—exploitation of children—violates fundamental human rights. As UNICEF put it: "Mobilizing society provides the best guarantee that a government will take its responsibilities seriously." Activism is "paying dividends all over the world."[15]

CHAPTER 7

CAMPAIGNING TO STOP
child LABOR

Activist organizations working to end child-labor abuses have been increasing in number and diversity since the early 1990s, and these groups can be found in all parts of the world. They include labor unions, religious groups, child-welfare organizations, human-rights groups, consumer organizations, and international agencies such as UNICEF.

The International Labor Organization based in Geneva, Switzerland, is one UN agency that has been especially active in keeping the issue of child exploitation before the world community. Since its inception in 1919, child-labor issues have been a top priority for the organization, and beginning in the early 1990s, the ILO stepped up its efforts to stop abusive child-labor practices. In 1992 the organization established the International Program on the Elimination of Child Labor (IPEC), which, at the request of national governments, has implemented more than 600 action programs in twenty-seven countries. The goal of these programs is to prevent and combat child labor by helping children withdraw from work in selected villages, provide support services for the children and their families, and change community attitudes toward child labor.

An IPEC program does not begin until a national government and the ILO sign a Memorandum of Understanding, which spells out areas of cooperation. Surveys are conducted to determine the child-labor problem in the country, which forms the basis for developing a national plan of action. No single organization or group carries out the plan. Rather, groups ranging from academic experts to labor organizations to media representatives work together through a coordinating committee. Part of IPEC's strategy is to gradually ease out of the picture after programs and policies are established so that local people can be in charge.

The ILO also initiated the Global March Against Child Labor, a campaign that began in early 1998 and included marches and other demonstrations in Asia, North America, Europe, Latin America, and Africa. In the United States the Robert F. Kennedy Memorial Center for Human Rights was one of the organizations helping to coordinate events. The march was designed to culminate during the June meeting of the International Labor Organization in Geneva. At the meeting, the ILO considered a new convention on child labor and mobilized worldwide efforts to protect and promote the rights of all children, especially the right to receive a free, meaningful education and to be free from economic exploitation.

While many UN activities are under way to stop exploitation of children, numerous other activist groups worldwide are working on local and regional projects. Only a small portion of such groups can be included here. But their activities represent the wide diversity of projects designed to tackle the complex problem of child labor.

GRASSROOTS ORGANIZING

In Pakistan the Bonded Labor Liberation Front (BLLF), which helped rescue such enslaved children as Iqbal Masih, is a grassroots organization that hopes to eventually eradicate bonded child labor in its country. The BLLF has saved thousands of children, but not without risk. Some of its members have been attacked by thugs working for carpet makers, and a few have been killed. The founder of the organization, Ehsan Ullah Khan, was charged with "economic treason" because BLLF supposedly undermined the carpet industry, and Khan was forced to leave his country.[1]

Child Workers in Asia (CWA) is a network of NGOs and individuals involved in the child-labor movement in various Asian countries. CWA was organized in the late 1980s because activists knew that the "most effective way to create change is through grassroots involvement and local advocacy." Thus CWA has held workshops to discuss the problems of working children and has established local groups in Nepal, the Philippines, Indonesia, and Thailand. The groups share information, experiences, problems, and ideas through consultations and exchanges across the region, and CWA publicizes the work of the organizations through a newsletter and other resources.

The Abrinq Foundation for Children's Rights in Brazil is another grassroots group. Abrinq encourages industries to enroll children in school rather than employ them as laborers. Oded Grajew, Abrinq's president and a former toy manufacturer, says that many Brazilian children work with their families in agriculture and also in charcoal production. The family receives a contract and "is paid by a company to achieve a certain level of production," Grajew explained, "but the company contracts the father or the mother for an amount of production that can be achieved only by having the children working."[2]

Children are also involved in some way in the production of such Brazilian exports as oranges, sugar, cars, shoes, clothing, and steel. Grajew noted that since the foundation was initiated, many companies have "made a commitment to eliminate child labor in the chain of production." But this was "always in response to pressure." The foundation began publicizing the names of companies linked to child-labor abuses, and because firms did not want their reputation tarnished by negative publicity, most quickly agreed not to buy from contractors and suppliers who employ children. They also pledged to help children in some way. In return, Abrinq allows companies to mark their products with a "Company Friend of Children" label. The foundation's efforts not only have helped raise awareness of children's issues in Brazil but also have encouraged an increasing number of children to enroll in school. In addition the foundation has conducted a campaign to raise public awareness "that if children are not at school, they are not prepared to have good jobs."[3]

Nevertheless, child labor is still widespread in Brazil, according to a Brazilian labor leader, Nelson Morelli, who was in the United States in January 1998. Morelli spoke to a rally of the International Brotherhood of Teamsters in Tampa, Florida, where union members were calling on U.S. juice companies such as Minute Maid, which uses concentrate from Brazilian orange groves, to certify that its products are child-labor free.[4]

KIDS HELPING KIDS

Some of the most effective grassroots efforts have been initiated by youth groups. Many young people are dynamic activists in the fight to bring public pressure to bear on child-labor abuses. Craig Kielburger of Thornhill, Ontario, Canada, for example, began his efforts on behalf of child-labor victims when he was only twelve years old. Kielburger had read about the tragic life of carpet weaver Iqbal Masih, who escaped bonded labor and helped free other children like himself in Pakistan. "I thought if he could do so much, that I should try to do something too," Kielburger told a reporter.[5] He began speaking about child labor at his school and eventually formed a group called Free the Children.

At the request of IPEC, the young Canadian traveled to Nepal, India, Pakistan, Thailand, and Bangladesh to see child-labor conditions firsthand. He was accompanied by a Canadian youth activist, Alam Charles Rahman, who was going to India to do volunteer work in the fight against child labor. Rahman escorted Craig on his trip, arranged for meetings at factories, set up press conferences, and filmed many interviews that Kielburger held with young workers. Kielburger later said that read-

Craig Kielburger, of Thornhill, Ontario, Canada, who decided to make a difference after reading an account of Iqbal Masih.

ing about child labor is quite different from actually talking to children face-to-face.

"You have to look into their eyes and see where they are working," he told a reporter. "I went to a brick kiln where children made bricks all day. I tried it, just to see how hard it was. I only did it a little while and was exhausted. I couldn't imagine children working at this all day." Describing the effects of the children's grim working environment, Kielburger reported:

> *I met children with arthritis in their hands, children with their hands severely cut. One girl I met worked at a metals factory; she showed me her severely burned arms and legs, which happened when she spilled some hot metals on herself. I met another eight-year-old girl who worked in a recycling factory in India, separating syringes from used needles. No protective clothing whatsoever. She never heard of AIDS; wore no gloves or shoes.[6]*

While in India, Kielburger also met fourteen-year-old Nageshwer, who had been freed from bonded labor. He had worked fifteen hours each day in a carpet factory to pay off money his grandfather had borrowed years ago. His body was covered with burn marks from a hot iron used to brand and punish workers. Another young carpet worker described the fate of two boys who escaped but were caught—as a lesson to the other workers, the boys were killed.[7]

When Kielburger returned home, he began a letter-writing campaign to free children from inhumane working conditions. Free the Children expanded with branches across Canada and in the United States and Switzerland. After Iqbal Masih was shot and killed in 1995, members of Free the Children became even more active, setting up a website on the internet, speaking to schools and community organizations, and raising funds to petition governments for an end to exploitation of children wherever they are in the world.

IQBAL MASIH'S LEGACY

In the United States, students at Broad Meadows Middle School in Quincy, Massachusetts, knew nothing about Free the Children when they heard the news of Iqbal Masih's death. But they were well aware of the horrors that Masih had experienced. The young activist had visited the middle school in December 1994, several months before his death, and he had made the plight of bonded children real. As one student, Kelly Mullen, noted after Iqbal's visit: "I never knew about 'bonded labor' before. It makes me feel lucky to live in the United States. When Iqbal told us about how he was beaten, and what he was beaten with, it brought tears to my eyes." Peter Coletti reported that he "felt really bad. He [Iqbal] was so small because of lack of food." Still another student, Kristen Fox, "was shocked to hear that kids are chained to looms in Pakistan. I think more now about things I take for granted."[8]

Iqbal also shared his dream with the middle-school students: He hoped to build a school in Muridke—his village; he wanted children to be free and educated. So

Broad Meadow seventh graders decided to honor Masih's memory by raising money to build a village school. Many people told the students that they had little chance to reach their goal, but the students were not discouraged. They immediately organized a Kids Campaign and created posters with messages such as "Iqbal, we'll keep on fighting" and "Iqbal's dream will live 4-ever" that were displayed in Copley Square in Boston a few days after Iqbal's death. Students also prepared items commemorating Iqbal's life, which were added to a time capsule to be opened in 2005.[9]

The public display was only the beginning, however. Students were determined to build a school in Pakistan. Led by two energetic students, Amy Papile and Amanda Loos, the campaign raised funds through bake sales, candy drives, and similar activities. With the help of language-arts teacher Ron Adams, social-studies teacher Donna Willoughby, and Scholastic Network in New York City, the students also campaigned on the internet. Scholastic maintains the nation's largest on-line system for teachers and students, and the Broad Meadow students were able to create their own website titled "A School for Iqbal—A Bullet Can't Kill a Dream."

Through their internet connection the Broad Meadow students contacted other middle schools across the United States to share the story of Iqbal. Soon classes were sending their contributions to the Kids Campaign, as were groups such as the Child Labor Coalition, UNITE, and the American Federation of Teachers. Various politicians and celebrities contributed also. And President Bill Clinton wrote to the students, pledging his support and that of his administration to "implement international child-labor protections." The president also praised the Broad Meadow students for their "courageous work" and expressed his hope "that your compassion will inspire others to reach out in a similar spirit of community and caring."[10]

By May 1996 the students had raised well over $100,000, and donations have continued to arrive from more than two dozen countries and all 50 states. In April 1996 the Kids Campaign formed a partnership with Sudhaar, a Pakistani human-rights organization that was able to build the "School for Iqbal" in Punjab Province, where Iqbal was born. The school opened in November 1996 for 200 of the poorest children who were either former bonded workers or at risk of being sold into bondage. A year later an update on the Kids Campaign website noted that "boys and girls attend classes daily with much cooperation and support from local community, government and business leaders. Parents are beginning to see education as an option" to damaging child labor. In addition, Sudhaar has established the Iqbal Masih Education Foundation, which will provide funds for operating the school in the years ahead.[11]

Iqbal's legacy goes beyond the successful school. The Kids Campaign has set up a new Online March Against Child Labor. This is a symbolic march, which will allow schools and youth groups to voice their opposition to child labor by posting messages on the internet.

OTHER STUDENT ACTIVISTS

As an increasing number of young people have learned about the issue of child labor, they have started numerous projects to do their part to stop exploitation. In 1996, for example, a group of students in a law and government class at Monroe High School in Los Angeles, California, campaigned to ban the purchase of soccer balls and other gear made with child labor. The students did not confine their activities to their own school. Rather they took on the nation's second-largest school district—the Los Angeles Unified School District (LAUSD), which purchases about 800 soccer balls each year. According to a *Los Angeles Times* editorial:

> *The Monroe students began their crusade as part of a class project. From there, they used the Internet to research conditions and contacted national and international human-rights organizations. Along the way, they petitioned elected officials. . . . Finally, the students were invited to address the board, which ordered an immediate halt to buying balls—or anything else—made by child workers.*[12]

On November 20, 1997, students in numerous countries rallied against child labor during the Universal Day of the Rights of the Child sponsored by the United Nations. In New Delhi, India, an estimated 2,000 children, including students in their school uniforms and former child laborers from remote villages, rallied and marched to protest child labor. One protester was eleven-year-old Washima Khatun, who said that "girls in my village do not study—they work. But I wanted to go to school." Washima's parents had "kept her home to help weave blankets," an AP report explained. Washima "still works mornings, but now . . . she attends classes in the afternoons run by a private development group. The group persuaded her parents she needed an education."[13]

In December 1997 the National Labor Committee in the United States sponsored Disney Week, and hundreds of young people took part. Among participants were members of the Girls Club in Sacramento, California, who dressed as Snow White's Seven Dwarfs and visited the Disney store to protest sweatshops. Countless other young people (as well as adults) wrote letters to the Disney Company expressing concern about the way a company—which receives numerous federal tax breaks and earns billions of dollars annually—exploits workers overseas.

Young people have also taken part in international conferences designed to call attention to child-labor abuses. In September 1997 a Regional Consultation Against the Most Intolerable Forms of Child Labor took place in Bangkok, Thailand. A Children's Forum was an important part of the Bangkok conference, providing an opportunity for working youth to speak for themselves about their concerns.

A seventeen-year-old factory worker, Chongruk Ngam-Im of Thailand, said she has been working in a Bangkok garment factory since she was thirteen. "Like other children, I have a family of my own, but we do not have the happiness of living together in the same house. My parents and two younger sisters live in a rural area, while I am living inside the Factory's hostel in Bangkok." Although she said her job was not too hard, she frequently has to work long hours and regrets that she has not had time to study or learn about the issues of child rights. In her view, child-labor meetings and conferences should include working children so that they have a voice and can discuss their problems.[14]

A fourteen-year-old Indonesian girl, Ida Narsidah, works in a biscuit factory in Tanerang. When she was just a youngster, her parents divorced, and she went to live with her grandfather. She had to drop out of school to go to work in order to support her grandfather and her four younger siblings. Along with about 100 other children between the ages of twelve and fifteen, Ida works at least ten hours per day. Her wish for the future is that "every child could go to school and would not have to do heavy jobs."[15]

Participants in the Children's Forum also prepared a statement on dealing with the most intolerable forms of child labor, including sexual exploitation of children, bonded and slavelike labor, and hazardous work. They recommended that parents, NGOs, and government organizations "work in equal partnership and in consultation with the working children" to stop the worst exploitation of children and also to help young people find acceptable work.

The statement noted the need to develop various types of campaigns with working children to raise public awareness of children's rights and child-labor issues. In addition, the youth group advocated punishing employers, especially abusive employers, who violate child-labor laws; setting up a monitoring system to ensure that working conditions improve; providing recovery programs for children rescued from damaging child labor and recreational activities and workshops for child workers still in factories who need to build self-esteem.[16]

Activists repeatedly issue the same message: Get children into school, provide jobs for adults, and help societies understand that exploiting children not only damages them but also violates their basic human rights. Yet no matter how many times the message goes forth, the complete elimination of child labor cannot be achieved in a short time. Reaching the goal will depend on actions from many segments of a nation and the worldwide community, as has been stated numerous times. Individuals who want to "do the right thing" are one component in the overall effort.

CHAPTER 8

DOING THE
"RIGHT THING"

With all the interrelated issues surrounding the exploitation of children worldwide, you might well wonder how a person can make socially responsible decisions. For example, you might want to buy a pair of sneakers, sporting equipment, jeans, a toy, orange juice, or some other product. Perhaps you are concerned that whatever you buy is going to help perpetuate the cycle of poverty for workers in developing countries. Should you refuse to buy a brand-name product that you suspect has been made by exploited workers? How do you find a substitute? What if you have to pay more for a product that is guaranteed child-labor free? Will it make any difference in the global scheme of things whether you make a "just" decision?

Other questions might also be raised. What effect can an individual have on a government or manufacturers in countries far away? Some activist campaigns have helped bring about small changes, but how can you take part? Should you help initiate a campaign in your own community? None of these questions can be answered easily. But a first step in determining what you can do is to become more informed by researching the many reports on exploitative child labor.

EDUCATION

Extensive information is available in these reports by the U.S. Labor Department: *By the Sweat and Toil of Children* (Volumes I and II) and *The Apparel Industry and Codes of Conduct: A Solution to the International Child Labor Problem?* The reports are free from the Child Labor Society, U.S. Department of Labor, and are also available on the DOL's website to anyone with internet access. Numerous other reports, such as UNICEF's annual *State of the World's Children*, are posted on the internet as well. Postal and internet addresses for the DOL and other organizations are listed at the back of this book.

A variety of organizations maintain websites that include information on exploitative child labor and suggestions for action to remedy the problem. These include the International Save the Children Alliance, the International Program for the Elimination of Child Labor, the Child Labor Coalition and its RUGMARK campaign, the National Child Labor Committee, the National Labor Committee, and Corporate Watch (CW). The last mentioned is not an organization as such. Instead, it is a website set up by the Institute for Global Communication and the Transnational Resource and Action Center.

According to CW's homepage, the site is designed to "harness the internet as a vehicle for action" and provide "everyday internet users, activists, journalists and policy makers" with tools "to investigate and analyze corporate activity."[1]

One site for young people, called ILO Kids, was set up by the International Labor Organization. UNICEF's Voices of Youth website provides interactive activities so young people can learn about issues affecting the welfare of children. Some schools are also offering an anti-sweatshop curriculum for students. In Newark, New Jersey, for example, students in grades 7 through 12 attending Catholic schools are receiving instruction on the history of U.S. labor laws, including laws that eventually made child labor and sweatshops illegal. Public schools in other states have offered similar components to social studies and other curricula.

MAKING
BUYING DECISIONS

Marymount University in Arlington, Virginia, home of a leading design school and the Center for Ethical Concerns, conducted surveys in 1995 and 1996 to tally consumer views on buying goods produced in sweatshops, which usually includes the employment of underage workers. Out of 1,023 adults surveyed in 1996, 83 percent said that if they knew a garment was not made in a sweatshop they would be willing to pay an additional $1 on a $20 item. A majority—79 percent in 1995 and 78 percent in 1996—indicated they would avoid shopping at a store that sold sweatshop-made garments.[2]

Other surveys have produced similar responses. Nevertheless, many consumers do not necessarily act according to their principles. In the first place, it may be too difficult to find out whether the sporting goods or other items you plan to buy are child-labor free. Some products, like soccer balls and some clothing, may carry a label indicating that manufacturers have not used child labor, but most often you will have to investigate to determine whether exploited children helped make a product. Chances are that salespeople will not know, but some organizations contend that buying goods with a Made-in-the-U.S.A. label will ensure that child labor has not been used. You can also check with the U.S. Department of Labor, which maintains a Trendsetters list of manufacturers and retailers who have pledged not to do business with sweatshops. The list is posted on DOL's website. Other groups that monitor companies for labor abuses include the AFL-CIO, Co-Op America, Corporate Watch, National Consumers League, and UNITE.

JOINING A CAMPAIGN

Thousands of young people have taken part in one or several campaigns, such as the Global March Against Child Labor. Ongoing activities are part of the Kids Campaign and Free the Children, and you can write to them or access their websites for updates. In addition, you can talk with your family and friends about exploitation of children and get them to join with you in your own efforts to spread the message about child-labor abuses.

The Child Labor Coalition's RUGMARK campaign is one more continuing effort. You can take part by developing a list of local stores that carry carpets with the RUGMARK label and sending the list to the CLC. The organization maintains a database of retailers who sell carpets with the RUGMARK label, which allows them to better respond to consumers who want to know where to buy child-labor-free carpets. CLC will provide details on this action program.

Letter-writing is a also a common campaign effort. Individuals or groups can write to manufacturers to inquire whether they use exploited labor and what they are doing to monitor production. Letters can also be sent to embassies in the United States, asking ambassadors of various countries how their nation protects children, what policies and programs are under way to stem exploitation, and whether the nation abides by the Convention on the Rights of the Child. When many individual letters accumulate, they can have an impact on government officials and other decision makers.

Contacting members of the U.S. Congress by mail, phone, or fax is another step you can take to express your views or to find out more about the global problem of child exploitation and also about protection for working youth in the United States. Senator Tom Harkin of Iowa and Representative George Miller of California, who are leading sponsors for the Child Labor Deterrence Act (S. 332 and H.R. 1301), welcome comments on their joint proposal. Representatives Tom Lantos and Christopher Smith of California and Barney Frank of Massachusetts along with about three dozen other representatives are also sponsors of proposed legislation to prevent exploitation of children.

THE CONTINUING FIGHT

Although eliminating conditions that lead to barbarous child-labor practices will be a long process, individuals and organizations around the world have been successful in calling attention to the scandal of child exploitation. Because of their work, there is a better understanding that child labor is not inevitable or irreversible. No one knows this better than children who have been freed from slavelike toil. One such child is Ranjeet, a former bonded worker in India, who gained his independence after more than three years of brutal eighteen-hour days in a carpet factory.

Ranjeet was rescued by Bachpan Bachao Andolan (BBA), which is part of the South Asian Coalition on Child Servitude. Ranjeet reported that when he was taken to the Mukti ashram for rehabilitation and study, he was "only twelve years old and very weak." But he is now "very active. My interest is to learn carpentry, and slowly, I have started to identify tools and make furniture also. My stay with Mukti *ashram* was for nine months from the 28th of November, 1996 to June 1997. Within this short period of time, I became self-sufficient. Nowadays, I am living in my village with my family."[3]

This type of positive ending to forced labor provides hope that someday barbaric exploitation of children will be seen globally as an intolerable practice. Carol Bellamy of UNICEF stated it this way: "As we step into the next millennium, hazardous child labor must be left behind, consigned to history as completely as those other forms of slavery that it so closely resembles."[4]

SOURCE NOTES

CHAPTER 1

1. "A Former Child Laborer's Shopfloor View: An Interview with Nazma Akhter," *Multinational Monitor* (January/February 1997), electronic version, no page number.
2. Ibid.
3. Stan Grossfeld, "Trapped in a Hellhole," *Boston Globe* (December 29, 1994), p. A8.
4. Ibid.
5. J. Patrick Slavin, "Haitian Children in Servitude" (January 1997), on the internet at http://www.unicefusa.org/issues97/jan97/haiti.html.
6. Elionardo, "Statements from the Working Children" (October 22, 1997), on the internet at http://www.loxinfo.co.th/~cwanet/state.htm.
7. International Labor Organization, "Oslo Conference to Seek Global Strategy for Combating Child Labor," press release (October 27, 1997).
8. Quoted in Reid Kanaley, "Marcy Abramson Shoemaker— She Puts Herself on the Line," *Philadelphia Inquirer* (March 2, 1997), magazine section, p. 6.
9. International Labor Organization, "Oslo Conference to Seek

Global Strategy for Combating Child Labor," press release (October 27, 1997).

10. Carol Bellamy, "State of the World's Children 1997," United Nations Children's Fund, on the internet at http://www.unicef.org or at gopher://gopher.unicef.org:70/00/.cefdata/.sowc97/sowc97.txt.

11. Child Labor Coalition, Executive Summary, "Model State Child Labor Law" (1993), on the internet at http://www.essential.org/clc/info/exec.html.

12. Ibid.

13. U.S. Department of Labor, "Country Profile of India," on the internet at http://www.dol.gov/dol/ilab/public/media/reports/sweat/india.htm.

14. Quoted in Jocasta Shakespeare, "Gardens of Shame" reprinted from *The Observer*, July 9, 1995, *World Press Review* (October 1995), electronic version, no page number.

15. Jocasta Shakespeare, "Gardens of Shame" reprinted from *The Observer*, July 9, 1995, *World Press Review* (October 1995), electronic version, no page number.

16. Quoted in Ibid.

17. S.L. Bachman, "Young Workers in Mexico's Economy: NAFTA Aims at Curbing Child Labor, But It's Rampant South of the Border," *U.S. News & World Report* (September 1, 1997), p. 40-41.

18. Carol Bellamy, "State of the World's Children 1997," United Nations Children's Fund, on the internet at http://www.unicef.org or at gopher://gopher.unicef.org:70/00/.cefdata/.sowc97/sowc97.txt.

CHAPTER 2

1. Carol Bellamy, "State of the World's Children 1997," United Nations Children's Fund, on the internet at http://www.unicef.org or at gopher://gopher.unicef.org:70/00/.cefdata/.sowc97/sowc97.txt.

2. Josh Kretman, "Reporter's Notebook," CE News Service Stories online (December 9, 1996) on the internet at http://www.ce.org/topnews/josh.htm.

3. Children's Express News Team, "Children Supporting Fami-

lies" (February 7, 1997), on the internet at http://www.ce.org/
topnews/bglwork.htm.

4. Taliinsar Dorjiin, *Children's Forum* (September 1-5, 1997)
on the internet at http://www.loxinfo.co.th/~cwanet/
talinsar.htm.

5. Rosemarie Gabot, *Children's Forum* (September 1-5, 1997)
on the internet at http://www.loxinfo.co.th/~cwanet/
rosemari.htm.

6. "Child Labor in Pakistan," *Atlantic Monthly* (February 1996),
electronic version, no page number.

7. Carol Bellamy, "State of the World's Children 1997," United
Nations Children's Fund, on the internet at http://
www.unicef.org or at gopher://gopher.unicef.org:70/00/
.cefdata/.sowc97/sowc97.txt.

8. Patralekha Chatterjee, "Children for Sale," *Chicago Tribune*
(April 27, 1997), Section 13, p. 1.

9. Bureau of International Labor Affairs U.S. Department of
Labor, A Report to Congress: *By the Sweat and Toil of Children*, Volume I (July 15, 1994) on the internet at http://
www.dol.gov/dol/ilab/public/media/reports/sweat/main.htm.

10. Ibid.

11. Carol Bellamy, "State of the World's Children 1997," United
Nations Children's Fund, on the internet at http://
www.unicef.org or at gopher://gopher.unicef.org:70/00/
.cefdata/.sowc97/sowc97.txt.

12. Ibid.

13. Bureau of International Labor Affairs U.S. Department of
Labor, *By the Sweat and Toil of Children*, Volume I, Executive Summary (July 15, 1994) on the internet at http://
www.dol.gov/dol/ilab/public/media/reports/sweat/summary.htm.

14. United Nations, *Preamble, Convention on the Rights of the
Child* (1989), on the internet at http://www.unicef.org/crc/
preamble.htm.

15. United Nations, *Part I: Substantive Provisions, Convention
on the Rights of the Child* (1989), on the internet at http://
www.unicef.org/crc/part1.htm.

16. Ibid.

17. Ibid.

18. International Labor Organization, International Program on the Elimination of Child Labor, IPEC: International Conference on Child Labor—Strategies for Eliminating Child Labor, synthesis document, International Conference on Child Labor, Oslo, Norway, October 27-30, 1997, on the internet at http://www.ilo.org/public/english/90ipec/others/conf/oslo/syn.htm.

CHAPTER 3

1. Kathlyn Gay and Martin K. Gay, *Heroes of Conscience* (Santa Barbara, CA: ABC-CLIO, 1996), pp. 259-261.
2. Sydney H. Schanberg, "Six Cents an Hour," *Life* (June 1996), electronic version, no page number.
3. Ibid.
4. Kailash Satyarthi, "Break the Chains—Save the Childhood" (August 1, 1996), on the internet at http://www.wizard.net/~friends/chain.htm.
5. Lee Tucker and Arvind Ganesan, "The Small Hands of Slavery: India's Bonded Child Laborers and the World Bank," *Multinational Monitor* (January/February 1997), electronic version, no page number.
6. U.S. Department of State, "1996 Human Rights Report: United Arab Emirates," released January 30, 1997.
7. "Children in Bondage," *World Press Review* (January 1996), pp. 8-9.
8. Carol Bellamy, "State of the World's Children 1997," United Nations Children's Fund, on the internet at http://www.unicef.org or at gopher://gopher.unicef.org:70/00/.cefdata/.sowc97/sowc97.txt.
9. Human Rights Watch/Asia, "Burma: Children's Rights" (January 16, 1997), on the internet at http://www-uvi.eunet.fr/human-rights/ebn24ja=26jan97-3.html.
10. John Pilger, " 'Death Railway' Revisited: Rebuilding with Slave Labor," *World Press Review* (September 1996), electronic version, no page number.
11. Bureau of International Labor Affairs U.S. Department of Labor, *By the Sweat and Toil of Children*, Volume II: The Use of Child Labor in U.S. Agricultural Imports & Forced

and Bonded Child Labor: A Report to the Committee on Appropriations U.S. Congress (October 11, 1995), on the internet at http://www.dol.gov/dol/ilab/public/media/reports/sweat2/bonded.htm.

12. Ibid.

13. Carol Bellamy, "State of the World's Children 1997," United Nations Children's Fund, on the internet at http://www.unicef.org or at gopher://gopher.unicef.org:70/00/.cefdata/.sowc97/sowc97.txt.

14. "The Story of Dhiraj K.C., A Child Domestic Worker in Nepal," *CWA Newsletter* (January-March 1997), on the internet at http://www.loxinfo.co.th/~cwanet/archive/c_v13n1/dhiraj.htm.

15. Madeline Eisner, "In Cambodia, Former Child Prostitutes Get a Chance to Dream Again," UNICEF feature (October 1996).

16. Ibid.

17. Carol Bellamy, "State of the World's Children 1997," United Nations Children's Fund, on the internet at http://www.unicef.org or at gopher://gopher.unicef.org:70/00/.cefdata/.sowc97/sowc97.txt.

18. Ibid.

19. M. O'Kane, "Death of Innocence," *The Guardian* (December 2, 1996), electronic version, no page number.

CHAPTER 4

1. "The Life of the Industrial Worker in 19th-Century England," on the internet at http://ab.edu/~delcol_l/worker.html.

2. Ibid.

3. Ibid.

4. George Brown Tindall, *America: A Narrative History*, Volume Two, second edition (New York: W.W. Norton & Company, 1988), p. 738.

5. Russell Freedman, *Kids at Work: Lewis Hine and the Crusade Against Child Labor* (New York: Clarion Books, 1994), p. 47.

6. Mary Van Kleek, "Charities and the Commons," report of

the National Consumers' League, the Consumers' League of New York City, the National and New York Child Labor Committees, and the College Settlements Association, January 18, 1908.

7. Ibid.

8. Marjorie Sarbaugh-Thompson and Mayer N. Zald, "Child Labor Laws: A Historical Case of Public Policy Implementation," *Administration & Society* (May 1995), electronic version, no page number.

9. Ibid.

10. United States Department of Labor Employment Standards Administration, Fact Sheet No. ESA 91-2.

11. Tom Lantos, "In Recognition of October 4, 1997—Day of Conscience to End Child Labor and Sweatshop Abuses," *Congressional Record* (October 2, 1997), p. E1918.

12. David Foster and Farrell Kramer, Associated Press, "Kids as Young as 4 Found at Work in U.S.," *Los Angles Times* (December 14, 1997), p. A1.

13. Ibid.

14. Joan M. Clay and Elvis C. Stephens, "Child-Labor Laws and the Hospitality Industry," *Cornell Hotel & Restaurant Administration Quarterly* (December 1996), electronic version, no page number.

15. Suzanne Kapner, "Child Labor Fines Taking A Bigger $$$ Bite," *Nation's Restaurant News* (August 12, 1996), electronic version, no page number.

16. "Restaurant Cited for Child Labor Violations," *St. Louis Post-Dispatch* (January 8, 1997), electronic version, no page number.

17. Child Labor Coalition, Executive Summary, "Model State Child Labor Law," (1993) on the internet at http://www.essential.org/clc/info/exec.html.

18. David Foster and Farrell Kramer, Associated Press, "Secret World of U.S. Child Labor," *San Jose Mercury News* (December 19, 1997), p. 1EE.

19. S.L. Smith, "In Harm's Way: Child Labor in the 90s," *Occupational Hazards* (November 1995), electronic version, no page number.

20. Ron Nixon, "Caution: Children at Work," *The Progressive*

(August 1996), electronic version, no page number.

21. Quoted in Ibid.

22. Child Labor Coalition, Executive Summary, "Model State Child Labor Law," (1993) on the internet at http://www.essential.org/clc/info/exec.html.

CHAPTER 5

1. David Bacon, "How Global Economy Promotes Child Labor," Pacific News Service online, May 30, 1996.

2. Carol Bellamy, "State of the World's Children 1997," United Nations Children's Fund, on the internet at http://www.unicef.org or at gopher://gopher.unicef.org:70/00/.cefdata/.sowc97/sowc97.txt.

3. Ibid.

4. Bureau of International Labor Affairs U.S. Department of Labor, *The Apparel Industry and Codes of Conduct: A Solution to the International Child Labor Problem?* (1996) on the internet at http://www.dol.gov/dol/ilab/public/media/reports/apparel/main.htm.

5. Ibid.

6. Quoted in Associated Press, "Kathie Lee Fights Back on Sweatshops," *Seattle Times* (May 2, 1996), p. A5.

7. Quoted in Nancy Gibbs, "Cause Celeb: Two High-Profile Endorsers Are Props in a Worldwide Debate Over Sweatshops and the Use of Child Labor," *Time* (June 17, 1996), electronic version, no page number.

8. Rosemary Feitelberg, "Anti-Sweatshop Nike: Just Do It," *Women's Wear Daily* (October 23, 1997), electronic version, no page number.

9. Statement prepared by Kathie Lee Gifford, Congressional Testimony House Subcommittee on International Organizations and Human Rights, July 15, 1996 on the internet at http://www.house.gov/international_relations/104th/chlbtes1.htm.

10. Sydney H. Schanberg and Jimmie Briggs, "Six Cents an Hour," *Life* (June 1996), electronic version, no page number.

11. Quoted in Bonnie DeSimone, "Visit Sews Up U.S. Athlete's Endorsement," *Chicago Tribune* (May 3, 1997), Section 1, p. 2.

12. Associated Press, "Sporting Goods Makers Join Team to Monitor Curbs on Child Labor," *San Jose Mercury News* (November 13, 1997), Business Section, p. 1C.

CHAPTER 6

1. David R. Henderson, "The Case for Sweatshops," *Fortune* (October 28, 1996), electronic version, no page number.
2. George Miller and Llewellyn H. Rockwell, Jr., "Should Consumers Hold U.S. Retailers Responsible for Child Labor Abroad? (pro and con symposium), *Insight on the News* (July 15, 1996), electronic version, no page number.
3. Ibid.
4. "Sweatshops May Offer Best Jobs, But Must Face Obligations," *Houston Chronicle* (July 22, 1996), electronic version, no page number.
5. Business Wire, "IMRA Survey Reveals that Consumers Hold Governments Accountable for Eliminating Sweatshops," press release (July 11, 1996).
6. Christine Elwell, "Corporate Codes of Conduct" (March 1997) on the internet at http://qsilver.queensu.ca/law/ courses/law538/codesmar.htm.
7. "Nike Puts Its Code of Conduct in the Pocket of Workers," Nike press release (September 16, 1997).
8. Eyal Press, "Breaking the Sweats," *The Nation* (April 28, 1997), electronic version, no page number.
9. "Gem River Announces 'No Child Labor' Certification," press release (January 28, 1998).
10. Business Wire, "Safe and Fair Work Places Around the World," press release (October 14, 1997).
11. Ibid.
12. Arthur Friedman, "New Sweatshop Law in N.J. Touted as Toughest in U.S.," *Women's Wear Daily* (August 6, 1996), p.13.
13. Quoted in Ibid.
14. Quoted in Arthur Friedman, "Ohio City Adopts Policy Refusing to Buy Goods Made in Sweatshops," *Women's Wear Daily* (February 21, 1997), p. 4.
15. Carol Bellamy, "State of the World's Children 1997," United

Nations Children's Fund, on the internet at http://www.unicef.org or at gopher://gopher.unicef.org:70/00/.cefdata/.sowc97/sowc97.txt.

CHAPTER 7

1. Mark Schapiro, "Children of a Lesser God," *Harper's Bazaar* (April 1996), electronic version, no page number.
2. "Battling Brazil's Child Labor Brutality: An Interview with Aded Grajew," *Multinational Monitor* (January/February 1997), electronic version, no page number.
3. Ibid.
4. "Child Welfare Rally Targets Juicemakers," *St. Petersburg Times* (January 13, 1998), Business Section, p. E1.
5. Quoted in "Free the Children: An Interview with Craig Kielburger," *Multinational Monitor* (January/February 1997), electronic version, no page number.
6. Ibid.
7. Mark Clayton, "Dynamic Teen Wins Support for Child Rights," *Christian Science Monitor* (April 26, 1996), international section, p. 1.
8. "Reflections on a Friend, Grade 7 Reflections on the December 2, 1994 Visit by Human Rights Hero, Iqbal Masih of Pakistan," on the internet at http://www.digitalrag.com/mirror/iqbal/broadmdw/visit/visit.html.
9. Pamela M. Walsh, "Slain Pakistani Child Crusader Honored," *Boston Globe* (April 30, 1995), electronic version, no page number.
10. President Bill Clinton, letters to students of Mr. Ron Adams's Class (April 11, 1996), on the internet at http://www.digitalrag.com/mirror/iqbal/support/images/clintonl.jpg.
11. "A School for Iqbal December 1997 Update," on the internet at http://www.digitalrag.com/mirror/iqbal/updates.html.
12. "Kids' Compassion for Kids," *Los Angeles Times* (December 29, 1996), Editorial, p. B15.
13. Associated Press, "Kids Rally Against Sweatshops," *Newsday* (November 21, 1997), p. A67.
14. Chongruk Ngam-Im, *Children's Forum* (September 1-5, 1997) on

the internet at http://www.loxinfo.co.th/~cwanet/chongruk.htm.

15. Ida Narsidah, *Children's Forum* (September 1-5, 1997) on the internet at http://www.loxinfo.co.th/~cwanet/ida.htm.

16. "Recommendations for Stopping the Most Unacceptable Forms of Child Labour," *Children's Forum* (September 1-5, 1997) on the internet at http://www.loxinfo.co.th/~cwanet/unacform.htm.

CHAPTER 8

1. Corporate Watch on the internet at http://www.corpwatch.org.

2. Joyce Barrett, "Public Is Looking A Tad More to Stores' Role in Sweatshops," *Women's Wear Daily* (November 27, 1996), p. 3.

3. Free the Children, "Child Laborers—FREED!" (no date), on the internet at http://www.freethechildren.org/ranjeet.htm.

4. Carol Bellamy, "Child Labor: Rights, Risks, and Realities," *The Rotarian* (September 1997), electronic version, no page number.

FOR FURTHER
INFORMATION

CHILD LABOR COALITION
c/o National Consumers League
1701 K Street, N.W. Suite 1200
Washington, D.C. 20006
Website: http://www.essential.org/clc/

CHILDREN'S EXPRESS
New York Bureau
19 West 21st Street, Suite 1001
New York, NY 10010
Phone: 212-741-4700
Website: http://www.ce.org

COALITION FOR JUSTICE IN THE MAQUILADORAS
3120 West Ashby
San Antonio, TX 78228
Phone: 210-732-8957

COMMUNITY AID ABROAD
156 George Street
Fitzroy, Melbourne, VIC 3065

Australia
Phone: 800-034-034 or 3-9289-9444
Website: http://www.caa.org.au/campaigns

COUNCIL ON ECONOMIC
PRIORITIES
30 Irving Place
New York, NY 10003
Phone: 800-729-4237
Website: http://www.accesspt.com/cep

CORPORATE WATCH
Website: http://www.corpwatch.org

FREE THE CHILDREN
16 Thornbank Road
Thornhill, Ontario L4J 2A2
Canada
Website: http://www.freethechildren.org

HUMAN RIGHTS WATCH
485 Fifth Avenue
New York, NY 10017-6104
Phone: 212-972-8400
Website: http://www.hrw.org/

INTERNATIONAL LABOR
ORGANIZATION (U.S.)
Child Labor Study Group
200 Constitution Ave., N.W., Room S-1308
Washington, DC 20210

United States Department of Labor
Website: http://usa.ilo.org/

INTERNATIONAL SAVE THE
CHILDREN ALLIANCE
Save the Children Fund
17 Grove Lane
London SE5 8RD
United Kingdom
Website: http://osaka.savechildren.or.jp/alliance/

KIDS CAMPAIGN
Broad Meadows Middle School
50 Calvin Road
Quincy, MA 02169
Website: http://www.digitalrag.com/mirror/iqbal/index.html

NATIONAL LABOR COMMITTEE
275 7th Avenue
New York, NY 10001
Phone: 212-242-3002
Website: http://www.nlcnet.org

SWEATSHOP WATCH
c/o Korean Immigrant Workers Advocates
2430 W. Third Street
Los Angeles, CA 90057
Phone: 213-738-9050
Website: http://www.bayscenes.com/npl/sw/swhompag.htm

UNITED NATIONS CHILDREN'S FUND
United States Committee for UNICEF
333 East 38th Street
New York, NY 10016
http://www.unicef.org

UNITED STATES DEPARTMENT OF LABOR
Office of Public Affairs
200 Constitution Ave., N.W., Room S-1032
Washington, DC 20210
Phone:202-219-8211
Website: http://www.dol.gov

UNITED STATES DEPARTMENT OF LABOR
BUREAU OF INTERNATIONAL LABOR AFFAIRS
ILAB Office of Public Affairs
200 Constitution Ave., N.W., Room S-5006
Washington, D.C. 20210
Phone: 202-219-6373
Website: http://www.dol.gov/dol/ilab

INDEX